STALIN'S WAR
SOVIET UNIFORMS & MILITARIA 1941–45
IN COLOUR PHOTOGRAPHS

STALIN'S WAR
SOVIET UNIFORMS & MILITARIA 1941–45
IN COLOUR PHOTOGRAPHS

LÁSZLÓ BÉKÉSI

Photographs by
GYÖRGY TÖRÖK

THE CROWOOD PRESS

First published in 2006 by
The Crowood Press Ltd
Ramsbury, Marlborough
Wiltshire SN8 2HR

www.crowood.com

© Lászlo Békési 2006
Photographs
© György Török 2006

All rights reserved. No part of this publication may be reproduced or transmitted in any form or by any means, electronic or mechanical, including photocopy, recording, or any information storage and retrieval system, without permission in writing from the publishers.

British Library Cataloguing-in-Publication Data
A catalogue record for this book is available from the British Library.

ISBN 1 86126 822 X
EAN 978 1 86126 822 8

Dedication
To the forgotten Soviet soldiers

Edited by Martin Windrow
Typeset by
Jean Cussons Typesetting,
Diss, Norfolk
Printed and bound by
Craft Print International Ltd,
Singapore

Contents

Preface 5
Introduction & Select Bibliography 6

The Road to World War II:
Cycles in Soviet Military Symbolism 8

The War Years:
NKVD Guard, GULAG Camps, Winter 1939/40 13
Mine Clearing, 1943 25
Women's Roles in the Great Patriotic War 30
Winter Camouflage Clothing 32
Pilotkas 37
Information-Gathering 41
One-Man Range-Finder, 1944 45
TR Field Periscope 47
Naval Infantryman, Murmansk, 1942 49
Partisan, 1942 57
Tactical manuals 60
Artillery Captain, Caucasus, 1942 68
Sub-Machine Gunner, 1942/43 71
DT Machine Gun Team, Stalingrad, early 1943 72
Rifles Officer, 1943 75
Cossack Major, Spring 1943 78
From Collar Patches to Shoulder Boards 84
Joint Soviet-Hungarian Patrol, 1944/45 88
General Officers, 1944 93
Tank Crewman, 1944 100
Mosin Rifles, Soldiers' Equipment & Small Kit 106
Officers' Visored Caps 111
NKVD Commanders 118
Self-Propelled Gun Crewman, 1945 122
DT & DP Machine Guns 124
Junior Lieutenant, Engineers, 1945 127
Traffic Regulator, Berlin, 1945 134
Documents & Ephemera 136

Preface

This book was partly inspired by destroyed or removed Soviet war memorials all over Central Europe; and also by the trenches that I saw in my childhood. Every winter I went sledging on a small hill above the banks of the River Danube; at that age I had no idea why it was called Soldiers' Hill, but when I grew up I understood. This was the end of the 'Attila Line', dug around Budapest in three belts in 1944 to defend the Hungarian capital against advancing Soviet troops; and I learned to recognize the zig-zag traces of forgotten strong-points.

Life has changed since then. Since 1989 the names of many streets and squares in Budapest have been changed; and with a single exception, all the Soviet liberation monuments have been destroyed, or relocated to somewhere far from the city centre. They have been simplified (some would say, degraded) into a tourist attraction or theme park. I call it a 'Statue and Monument Concentration Camp', since they were forced to move, they are guarded and enclosed by fences, they will probably never leave, and in the meantime – like classic forced labourers – they make profits for some company.

Today's history books are being rewritten, too, and there is debate about the role of the Red Army. But once, on a TV programme, I heard about a letter from an old Russian lady who used to travel to Budapest to visit her father's name on a liberation monument near the place where he fell in 1944. When she came for the last time in 2004, the names of the fallen Soviet soldiers had disappeared – the wall was polished smooth, as if they had never been. In my hometown of Dunakeszi near Budapest the Soviet monument was also destroyed, and two other wall plaques were removed. These plaques had been erected in memory of victims of the Nazis, who had been tortured and killed in the town hall and the police headquarters – because of their origin, or because of their beliefs. There have been many changes in the world since 1945; but I believe that obliterating our history in this way is neither honest nor healthy.

On 4 April 2005, the 60th anniversary of the liberation of Hungary from the Nazis, there were no celebrations: it was a day of silence – the broadcast news did not even mention the anniversary. Whatever the suffering since that day, I believe that we have forgotten it too quickly. So in this book I would like to remember all the victims of World War II, and especially those neglected and now forgotten young Soviet soldiers whose names have been polished off the monuments. May they rest in peace.

LB
Budapest
9 May 2005

A private of the Red Air Force, 1941. Do not search for any significant details in his uniform – look at the boy. He was probably 14 or 15 years old.

Introduction

This is the third of my series of books for The Crowood Press on Soviet uniforms and militaria, which should be seen as a single sequence. The first part (*Soviet Uniforms and Militaria 1917–1991*, published 2000, referred to in this text hereafter as **SUM**) explains and illustrates the uniforms, insignia, ranks, awards and equipment of the Red (later Soviet) Army; the Navy (Fleet) – including Naval Infantry and Naval Aviation; the Air Force, and Paratroopers. The second book (*KGB & Soviet Security Uniforms and Militaria 1917–1991*, published 2002, hereafter **KSSUM**) deals with the history of the organisations and agencies of the Committee for State Security and the Ministry of Internal Affairs: the Militia (police), NKVD and later KGB, Frontier Guards, Internal Forces, OMON, Spetznaz, Prison and Customs services, Court personnel, and emergency services such as the Fire Brigade.

Since an extraordinary variety of uniforms and equipment were used by the Red Army during the Great Patriotic War, 1941–45 (as World War II was termed in the Soviet Union), I have focused in this volume on field uniforms and equipment especially of the period 1943–45 – seen all over the eastern and central European theatre of war from the end of the battle for Stalingrad right up to final victory in Berlin – since these have become the central interest of historians, collectors and re-enactment groups. The present volume is thus a natural extension and companion to the World War II sections in **SUM**, to which several cross-references will be found; readers will find it helpful to keep that book to hand while studying this one.

The subject is introduced by comments on a number of rare pre-war and early war items, some of which will help to clarify the evolution of the military symbolism seen in the later years. The original Imperial symbols were rejected after the Revolution in favour of others representing modernity and internationalism; but from early 1943 a new cycle restored some of the traditional Imperial symbols of national identity, celebrating neglected Tsarist heroes once again as a focus of loyalty and patriotism. Another feature of this book will be identified in contrasts between the strict official regulation of uniforms, and the actuality, which was sometimes very different. Such deviations reflected the soldiers' creativity and skills of adaption at times of widespread shortages of issue items and materials.

Since the previous volumes included my address and e-mail (see back cover flap), I have received many helpful and encouraging messages from fellow researchers – and some equally valuable corrections. (A few days before I finished this text an old and highly respected Hungarian military historian took me to task over the reconstructed photographs of NKVD officers in my second book: he insisted that NKVD personnel never polished their boots as smartly as we had shown...) Readers of the present volume are freely invited to contact me with information and queries.

A couple of points on style and terminology: in this text, Russian letters (for example, those displayed on some shoulder boards) are given in the Latin equivalents of the original Cyrillic alphabet, for the convenience of those who do not speak Russian. The colour of Red Army field uniform was described in Russian as 'olive'; there were wide variations in the actual shades of this *zashchitniy tsvet*, between olive-green, pea-green, mid- and dark-brown, and pale sand-khaki; in this text I refer simply to 'khaki', in the English use of the term, which approximates to a brownish US olive drab. The soldier's *shinel* greatcoat, by contrast, was often of a distinctly grey-brown shade.

ACKNOWLEDGEMENTS

I would like to express my thanks to the following, who patiently gave up their time to model for the photographs in this book: Zoltán Csaba, Zoltán Dósa, Balázs Jásdi, Monika Nyul, Sergei Naumovich Semyonov, György Somodi and Zoltán Vass; also Koichiro Ikezawa and Raizuke Hirasawa of the Tokyo Red Army Re-enactment Group; and the Czech Soviet Re-enactment Group. My thanks also, for his friendly advice over the years, to Prof Dr István Kajtár.

SELECT BIBLIOGRAPHY AND FURTHER READING

In English:
László Békési, *Soviet Uniforms & Militaria 1917–1991 in Colour Photographs*, The Crowood Press, 2000
László Békési, *KGB & Soviet Security Uniforms & Militaria 1917–1991*, The Crowood Press, 2002
Laszlo Békési, 'The Return of Tsarist Symbols in the Great Patriotic War', Sociology PhD dissertation
M.Degtyarev, V.Krylov & A.Kulinsky, *The Weapons of Kalashnikov*, exhibition catalogue, The Artillery Museum, St Petersburg, n.d.
V.A.Durov, *Russian and Soviet Military Awards*, Order of Lenin State History Museum, 1990
M.Furlan, *Soviet Army Insignia 1917–1985*, Military House, Toronto, 1988
O.V.Haritonov, *Soviet Military Uniform and Insignia*, Alga-Fund, St Petersburg, 1993
Vladimir Karpov, *Russia at War 1941–45*, Vendome Press, New York, 1987
I.I.Likhitskiy, *Art of Russian Miniature*, badge catalogue, Udacha, Lvov, 1995
Andrew Mollo, *Naval, Marine and Air Force Uniforms of World War II*, Blandford Press, Poole, 1975
Andrew Mollo, *The Armed Forces of World War II*, Orbis, London, 1981
G.A.Putnikov, *Orders and Medals of the USSR*, Novosti, Moscow, 1990
Henry Sakaida, *Heroes of the Soviet Union 1941–45*, Osprey (Elite No.111), Oxford, 2004
Henry Sakaida, *Heroines of the Soviet Union 1941–1945*, Osprey (Elite No.90), Oxford, 2003
A.Shalito, I.Savchenkov & Andrew Mollo, *Red Army Uniforms of World War II*, Windrow & Greene (Europa Militaria No.14), London 1993 (subsequently The Crowood Press)
Steven Zaloga, *Red Army of the Great Patriotic War 1941–45*, Osprey (Men-at-Arms No.216), London, 1989

In Russian:
V.M.Galaiko, *Symbols of the Nation*, Voyenizdat (Ministry of Defence Publishing Company), Moscow, 1990
P.P.Ganitchev, *Military Ranks*, DOSAAF (Friends of the Soviet Army & Navy Press), Moscow, 1989
I.A.Horobrih & A.S.Domank, *Insignia of Military Bravery*, DOSAAF, 1990
G.A.Kolesnikov & A.M.Rozhkov, *Orders and Medals of the USSR*, Voyenizdat, 1983
V.D.Krivtzov, *Variations (Collectors' Guide)*, Parts 1 & 2, Moscow, 1995 & 1996
V.V.Lavrentiev & P.D.Kazakov, *The Great Patriotic War*, Voyenizdat, 1984
Pavel Lipatov, *East Front Red Army and Wehrmacht Uniforms*, Technika-Mologiezhdi, Moscow, 1995
N.V.Ogarkov (ed), *Soviet Military Encyclopedia*, Vols 1–8, Ministry of Defence, Moscow, 1980
A.Volodin & N.Merlai, *Medals of the USSR*, Petchatniy Dvor, St Petersburg, 1997
A.B.Zhuk, *Handbook of Firearms*, Voyenizdat, 1993

(**Above**) *Students' identity cards. Leningrad, 2 June 1941: a young girl's student card for her forthcoming studies in the Leningrad Academy of the Peoples' Committee of Forestry; she was due to attend the Forest Engineering & Economy faculty from September. Kiev, 26 June 1941: a note in an army officer's student book, that he is soon to start his third-year studies to become a doctor, at the Kiev Medical Institute of the Peoples' Committee for Health.*

Both these students were probably happy and successful in June 1941; they enjoyed the advantages of a social mobility at least matching that in any society in the world at that date, where the sons and daughters of manual workers and illiterate peasants could attend schools, high schools and universities. However, these dates in June 1941 are the last entries in their student cards; they never went back to school to finish their studies. That month the greatest conflict in modern history broke out between the world's most powerful and ruthless ideological dictatorships, for lebensraum *and geo-political power, and swept away forever the lives planned by tens of millions of men and women.*

(**Right**) *Soldiers' personal books of the Great Patriotic War, 1941 – the equivalent to a Western soldier's paybook. These documents were of the cheapest quality, and lacked any decorative symbols other than the red star. The ranks were quickly filled with new volunteers and conscripts in the second half of the year 1941. The paybooks carried no photograph – there was no time, or film, to take millions of photographs within a few months. The books contain the simplest notes, and list the simplest equipment issue: each man was given one pair of short boots, a belt, an ammunition pouch, a* pilotka *cap, a* gymnastiorka *shirt-tunic and a pair of trousers. Perhaps 30 million men and women received such documents during the war; at least 11 million of those never returned home – and those are only the known killed and missing. Of the roughly 6 million taken prisoner, well over half died in captivity.*

The Road to World War II:
CYCLES IN SOVIET MILITARY SYMBOLISM

The Soviet war effort, and the visible symbolism displayed by Soviet uniforms, drew upon two totally different traditions: that of the former Imperial Russia, and that of the new Soviet state. Initially Soviet war propaganda was based upon the heritage of the 1917 Revolution and the Red victory in the Civil War of 1917–22. The population were encouraged to fight, and to exert themselves in every field of national activity, to defend the 'heroic achievements of the proletariat'. But soon after the outbreak of war, with its initial disastrous defeats, the Soviet leadership were forced to recognize that this Communist propaganda was failing.

There was an abysmal communications gap between the ideologically motivated leadership and the average citizens of the USSR – in fact, there were two wholly different Soviet Unions. The official identity of the nation was embodied in the images promoted by the Communist leadership: modernisation and industrialisation, symbolised by hydro-electric power plants (which were depicted in many Communist orders and certificates); modern cities, inhabited by the loyal masses of Communist workers and convinced intellectuals; and country villages, where the cheerful, productive labourers of the Kolkhoz collective farms enjoyed the benefits of electricity and Stalinets tractors.

The other, wholly separate Soviet Union was the daily reality faced by the long-suffering subjects of the ruthless dictatorship of the Party. These survivors of successive decades of ruinous civil war, widespread famine, and most recently of merciless and almost mindless purges, lived mentally in a Russia that drew its strength to endure from age-old traditions: depending on their background and education, from the Eastern Orthodox faith, folksongs and folktales, the Cossack tradition and a deep love of nature, or from the legacies of famous classical writers and painters, the Russian ballet, and the beauties of St Petersburg. The psychological power of the red star and hammer-and-sickle, and that of the Orthodox cross, co-existed in Soviet society.

With the realisation that the masses could not be sufficiently stirred by appeals based on the Communist ideology of which their actual experience was often contradictory, from at least early 1943 onwards the leadership turned back to pre-Revolutionary language and symbolism. Patriotic speeches, posters, films, the names of warships and military academies, the titles and designs of awards – all saw a revival of the cults of medieval and later Russian heroes; and certain features of Tsarist military uniform, discarded – even reviled – in the Revolution were also revived. From 1943 the churches were also re-opened, and priests were instructed to encourage the population.

This was no longer the war of the Communist Party, but a patriotic, nationalist war for the Motherland – a Great Patriotic War, as in the time of Napoleon's invasion. A former Imperial hero and later Tsarist military attaché in Paris, Alexei Alexeyevich Ingatiev, was appointed to head the Voyenizdat military publishing company, controlling written propaganda from late 1942. Boris Mihailovich Shaposhnikov, a deeply religious former hero of World War I, became a Marshal of the Soviet Union. Icons were carried in religious processions in Leningrad, Moscow and Stalingrad; priests wrote leading articles for the front page of *Pravda* and gave broadcast radio talks. The pictures on these pages illustrate some of the roots of this revived Russian patriotism – an ideology whose contribution to eventual victory was as important as the Red Army's tanks and artillery.

(Left) A postcard showing Stalin with Marshal Klimenti Voroshilov in the Kremlin, late 1930s. Note the contrast between their costumes, which may be described as representing on the one hand a 'pure' revolutionary form, and on the other a colourful military style following 'bourgeois, nationalist' norms. Stalin wears a version of the simple soldiers' coat as used since the Revolution, closed by hooks and with no insignia or visible buttons. Voroshilov displays the uniform of a Marshal of the Soviet Union introduced from 1935, with large red and gold insignia, and spurred riding boots. Later Stalin would also follow the colourful, decorative line, with his white summer uniform and gold lace shoulder boards.

(Right) *Patriotic spirit: an Imperial Fabergé cigarette case, made in St Petersburg, 1914. This fine machined-silver and enamel case bears the Tsar's crown and one of Nicolai II's mottoes: 'Loyalty, Bravery and Belief'. It was presented by the Tsar to honour an officer of proven courage and loyalty during the first year of World War I. The custom of giving art objects as military rewards had a long history in Russia, dating from the Middle Ages. In Imperial times these included jubilee coins, swords, daggers, trumpets, gorgets and goblets, and later* shashka *sabres, pistols and banners. Such specially manufactured and individually personalised items were at least as greatly treasured as the usual awards of medals and orders. This case bears (below) a silver hallmark, the double-headed Imperial eagle, and the initials of the Fabergé company's workmaster Fedor Afanasiyev.*

(Left) *Patriotic spirit: Imperial Russian Army enlisted man's cap, c.1916. This is the lightweight type made for summer use in the latter part of World War I. The material is of the same quality as used for flour bags, and the cap is reinforced inside the band with folded newspaper. This* furashka *was the most common headgear worn by both sides in the Civil War, with the Romanov cockade (orange, black and white, reading outwards) removed from those used by the Red armies and retained by the Whites. The orange and black Imperial colours were seen again in Soviet times: in the ribbons of the World War II Order of Glory and Victory over Germany medal, and on Guards naval cap tallies. The traditional oval became the 'new' shape of Soviet officers' cap badges in every branch and service from 1955.*

One way of dating unknown early 20th century Russian items is close study of any lettering; after the Revolution the Cyrillic alphabet was simplified, so earlier texts include various letters that were discontinued in 1918.

(**Left**) *Revolutionary spirit: personalised items of a Civil War veteran. Protective cases for pocket watches were popular during this period. In 1918 the first version of the Order of the Red Banner had a screw back rather than a suspension ribbon, although the screw post was sometimes worn through a red ribbon cockade. Originally most bore 'RSFSR' on the lower scroll, for the Russian Soviet Republic. Other republics initially awarded versions with their own national symbols, and even languages; before the Revolution several Central Asian peoples used the Turkish or Arabic alphabet, though later all accepted Cyrillic except for Armenia. After the Soviet Union was created, from 1 August 1924 the Order was made only in this single version with the legend 'SSSR'. From 1943 the Order was suspended on a ribbon of equal red-white-red stripes, with narrow white edges. The Red Banner and several other orders could be given collectively, to groups of workers (e.g., the* Pravda *editorial board – thus the display of the decoration on the cover masthead of that paper) and to units of the armed forces.*

(**Right**) *Internationalism: MOPR, the International Organisation for Helping the Fight of Revolutionaries, was established in 1922 – when the Civil War was still raging, but the Soviet leadership felt secure enough to extend its reach into the ideological struggle abroad. This badge, from 1928, symbolises a political prisoner waving a red cloth from a barred jail window. MOPR also used symbols of anti-racism, solidarity, and the globe breaking its chains. The USSR negotiated the release to Russia of political prisoners in several countries – for example, Mátyás Rákosi, head of the Hungarian Communist movement, after his involvement in the Spanish Civil War.*

(**Left**) *During 1918–22 the first official Revolutionary symbol of the Workers' and Peasants' Red Army (RKKA) was the hammer-and-plough on a red star, representing the unity of urban proletariat and peasant farmers and displayed on breast badges and – as here – on buttons and cap badges; the red enamel surface has long ago worn off this cap star. Note that the star shape is rather squatter than in later insignia. The hammer-and-sickle motif was first seen on the rank patches worn on the lower sleeve from 1919.*

(**Above**) Seen here with Red Army soldiers' books, as issued in the 1920s to active and reserve personnel of the RKKA, are examples of the first RKKA sleeve patches. These designs, variously coloured and detailed, were introduced gradually for various types of unit from 1919. Here, crossed rifles and raspberry-red identify infantry (which throughout this text will be referred to by the Russian term, 'rifles'; crossed sword and rifle and blue, convoy troops; and black, convoy troops headquarters. Embroidery was yellow for most units; gold embroidery was allowed for those awarded the Order of the Red Banner, and silver was a distinction for wounded soldiers, or battle-tested veterans with more than one year's service in the Civil War. Artillery had a bullet-shaped black patch with crossed cannons; cavalry, a horseshoe-shaped blue patch with crossed sabres. All these and other patches (for drivers, engineers, military court personnel, etc.) shared the rising sun motif and the red star.

The diamond shape always had an important role in Red Army symbolism. From four to one enamel diamonds were displayed on the collar patches of general officer equivalents by Army, Corps, Division and Brigade Commanders. It was seen before 1914 in the sleeve patch of railway troops; in that of World War II anti-tank artillery (see page 19); by both Militia and Army traffic regulation personnel (see **KSSUM**, page 38), and post-1945 by paratroopers, by tank troops as a field breast patch (see **SUM**, page 97), and in academy graduation badges.

Sleeve patches were worn on the upper left arm throughout most of the Soviet period, with some exceptions in the 1980s; leading seamen's and commissars' stars and NKVD sleeve patches of World War II were worn on both arms. Most of the branch-of-service colours which appeared from 1919 remained unchanged for more than five decades: dark blue for cavalry, raspberry-red for rifles, green for frontier guards, black for artillery and tank troops, light blue for the Air Force, etc. The system of colours was simplified only in 1969–70.

(**Below**) Red Air Force (VVS) sleeve patch, 1922. The winged star in silver was displayed by Air Force personnel other than pilots (who wore black wings) and observers (gold wings).

(Above) Early armoured troops collar badge, 1922–23. This combines the winged wheel, for mobility, with a lightning bolt, and the shield and broadsword recalling medieval heavy cavalry. Since the shield and sword were also chosen as the symbols of the state security organisation in the same period, the armoured badge was soon modified, and from 1924 onwards various tank-shaped collar symbols were used instead.

(Above left) Service regulations, 1920s. The first service regulations were published with a foreword by Mikhail Frunze, a hero of the Revolution and Civil War. Political education was always regarded as equal in importance with military knowledge and training.

(Left) Sleeve patch of a Navy gunnery electrician. It is not known when the wide range of naval specialist patches were introduced, but they were first mentioned in the 1934 naval uniform regulations. Such sleeve patches, originally marking qualification in various disciplines, had been worn in the Imperial Navy from 1881, and at that time a similar patch to this one identified sailors working with electical batteries (galvaner in Russian, after the early galvanic electric cell batteries). Since naval patches lacked any ideological symbols the Imperial patterns were replaced only gradually, such changes referring to technological innovations. Some World War II examples will be found on page 56.

The War Years

Although the Great Patriotic War officially broke out on 22 June 1941, is it meaningful to wonder whether it actually began at some earlier point – say, with the attempted Japanese invasion of Mongolia in 1938? Or the Nazi-Soviet partition of Poland in September 1939? The Soviet Union was always, in a sense, at war with opponents outside or inside its territory from the 1917 Revolution onwards. If they faced no other enemies, then the Communist authorities created them: 'rich peasants', 'counter-revolutionary saboteurs', racial minorities, intellectuals – or they simply fought against nature, by trying to drive canals and harness rivers.

NKVD GUARD, GULAG CAMPS, WINTER 1939/40

The Soviet Peoples' Committee for State Security (NKVD) saw various changes in its organisation and title, finally becoming the KGB long after World War II, in March 1954 (see **KSSUM***). The NKVD was a complex state-within-a-state, controlling almost everything from border security to the fire brigade, from the police to the bureau of statistics, from prisons and labour camps to the security of major industrial sites. As head of the NKVD the feared and hated Lavrenti Beria was almost as powerful as Stalin (over whose dead body he had little time to gloat in 1953, before his colleagues prudently had him executed himself).*

In cold weather various sheepskin coats were worn on top of the shinel *greatcoat, of different lengths and shades (white, black or mixed fleece) and with different collar designs. Buttons might be brass or earlier white metal types, with or without the hammer, sickle and star motifs; or of simple bone or bakelite, in large sizes (as here) convenient for gloved fingers.*

This was the last winter of official use of the budionovka *cloth helmet, although not in actual practice. In the second half of 1940 both Red Army and NKVD troops gradually began replacing it with the fleece-lined and fleece-flapped* ushanka *hat which gave better insulation; the* budionovka *had proved inadequate during the 1939 Winter War against Finland. Nevertheless, like several other obsolete items, the* budionovka *was still seen in the front lines in limited numbers right up to the spring of 1945.*

This guard's weapon is the 7.62mm M1891/30 Mosin Nagant rifle. For details of the different models in use during the war see pages 106–109.

NKVD GUARD, GULAG CAMPS, WINTER 1939/40

The two versions of the budionovka (or shlem) shown here are a light grey Red Army issue (**above left**), its original shade probably being the 'steel-grey' preferred by armoured troops; and an NKVD version (**above**). Generally the taller 'spire' of the latter example indicates earlier manufacture. The Army cap is a rare field example which lacks the traditional cloth star badge backing. The NKVD example is easy to recognize by the 'brick-red' shade of the cloth star – as used for collar patches and the bands of visored (peaked) caps exclusively by the internal security troops. Both these examples have small-sized regulation buttons of blackened finish bearing the star, hammer and sickle, and larger-sized brass badges filled with red enamel. Note the arrangement of the ear flaps for cold weather. The flaps of the budionovka and later ushanka could only be worn down by direct permission of commanding officers when the temperature dropped below −10°C (14°F).

(**Left**) An old brass petrol lamp, as used by guards, patrols and railway troops. Only a very small number of battery-operated torches (flashlights) were available for issue, and in wartime captured German examples were prized.

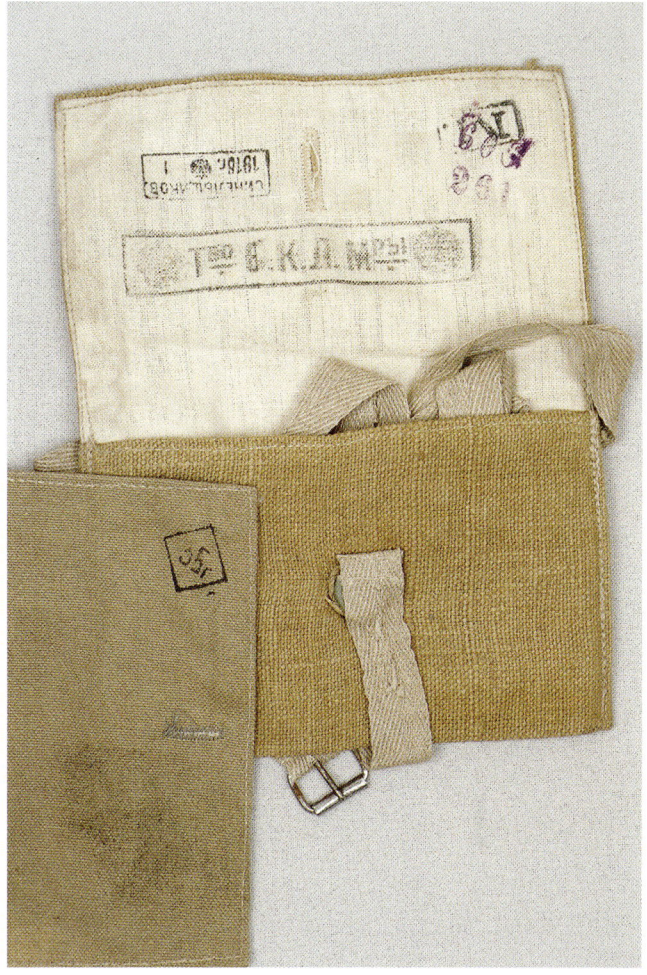

(Above left) Imperial emergency ammunition pouch, 1916. Due to the shortages of all kinds of equipment, left-over stocks of outdated and often poor-quality Imperial Army items were re-issued during the 1920s, 1930s, and especially during World War II. (The budionovka itself, thought to be a typically Soviet item, was in fact originally made for the 300th anniversary parades of the Romanov dynasty in 1913.) This pouch was made for the Imperial Army in 1916; it is of very poor material, little better than sackcloth, but the traditional leather belt pouches were not being produced in sufficient quantities due to shortages of time, leather and skilled workers alike. Imperial Army pieces held in stock were restamped from the second half of the 1930s (this example, in 1935) and were re-issued, particularly to guard troops such as convoy escorts, the NKVD VOHR sentries at industrial plants, camp guards throughout the huge 'GULAG archipelago', and later to guards at PoW camps. Even so, the large Imperial one-piece leather cartridge boxes for the Mosin rifles were also often seen in use during the first part of the war.

(Above) Note the variety of stamps on these examples. Usually stamps of the Imperial and early Soviet periods faded or disappeared after several washings; dates, factory identification and quality control marks are hard to find today in clothing or cloth equipment. Stamps which appear too distinct could be a sign of later faking.

(Left) Close-up of Imperial Army stamps. These show the date August 1916; the Imperial arms above crossed swords (Army quality control); and the stamp of the Russian company 'Mars'.

(Left) Studio portrait of a cavalry enlisted man, 1940–41, posing in a khaki *budionovka,* the khaki *gymnastiorka, dark blue breeches and high boots.* The *budionovka* has the low 'spire' of a late economy model; its red enamelled star is set on a cavalry-blue cloth star. Note the fly front and long length of the *gymnastiorka;* this fall-collar version was in use from 1935 until the introduction of shoulder boards from January 1943. Snipers were allowed to add a vertical raspberry-red stripe along the edge of the fly flap from 1937 until the 1943 reforms.

The collar patches are hard to explain. Under magnification they show the normal black edge-piping, but also a broad central stripe of a lighter shade than the basic cavalry-blue. The November 1940 regulations introduced a black central stripe for junior NCOs; but this soldier's patches lack the centrally-placed red-enamelled triangles of NCO ranks. They also lack the regulation cavalry branch badge, of crossed sabres set on a horseshoe, which should be pinned centrally at the rear end for all ranks; they bear instead only the brass triangle in the upper rear corner, introduced for all ranks as a levelling guide under the November 1940 regulations.

At the beginning of the war soldiers had few decorations to display, and often wore instead marksmanship or sports awards, or those from the Red Cross or chemical and air defence organisations *(Osoaviakhim).* Note the leather cavalry equipment, with a single-claw buckle, two shoulder braces, and the attached *shashka* sabre. An alternative was to sling the sword directly from a single narrow cross strap over the right shoulder.

(Right) Winter 1940/41: in this transitional period both the *budionovka* and the new *ushanka* were used by all branches and ranks. Note that both these examples are in new condition. Both soldiers wear the 1935 regulation raspberry-red collar patches with the rifles branch badge of crossed rifles set on a white-enamelled target.

(Above right) A reconstruction of infantry soldiers of the period, in *budionovka and shinel. The left hand man wears puttees with laced* ankle boots – as often issued for lack of the traditional high boots – belt pouches for rifle ammunition, and a simple bag-like backpack with canvas shoulder and chest straps. The lozenge-shaped collar patches for greatcoats – here, raspberry-red with black upper edges and the rifles branch badge – were not always worn. This scene is plausible for Asiatic troops of the Red Army's eastern commands. (Courtesy Japanese Red Army Re-enactment Group, Tokyo)

(**Left**) VOHR button, M1934. The Voyennizirovannaya Okhrana, 'Militarised Guard', were part of the NKVD security organisation, with responsibility for guarding important factories, power stations, stores and so forth. The members were usually retired policemen or soldiers, and the VOHR bore some similarity to a 'Home Guard'. Their uniform and insignia changed from time to time, but a constant was dark green distinctions – as piping on uniforms and pilotka caps, the bands of visored caps, or collar patches. From 1934 their distinctive cap badge featured crossed rifles – sometimes, as on this early white metal button, with fixed bayonets. Some NKVD specialist VOHR units – harbour guards, forest guards and convoy escorts – had their own insignia and uniforms.

From 1923 brass-coloured buttons were used only by very senior commanders – e.g. the commanders of military educational institutes. All more junior ranks of the Red Army, Militia, and other armed organisations used white metal buttons until 1935, when there was a general replacement with yellow metal buttons for all services. During wartime, dull iron or black-painted buttons were used once again, for lack of brass and for low visibility. Sometimes garments will be found with a mixture of Red Army and VOHR buttons, used simply when available.

(**Above**) Medals instituted in 1938, for 'Outstanding Achievements in Labour', and 'For Military Bravery'. Together with the medal for the '20th Anniversary of the Red Army' of the same year, these were the first of dozens of medals awarded by the Communist state for various achievements. The medal for bravery would be awarded some 5 million times. The first versions were worn on these simple red ribbons, deliberately avoiding any similarity with those of the Imperial past. Following the 1943 uniform reforms, all existing and later medals were issued with Imperial-type multi-coloured ribbons folded into the traditional five-sided shape (see pages 136–137).

Among the first recipients of the 'Outstanding Achievements in Labour' medal were the members of the Red Army's Alexandrov Song and Dance Ensemble, on the tenth anniversary of the troop's formation in the Far East Military District to entertain soldiers far from home. Alexander V.Alexandrov was the composer of the Soviet Anthem, and his ensemble was the most famous artistic group in the USSR. At first with only 12 members, it later grew to some 400 musicians, singers and dancers, and subsequently travelled the world. Their programme typically opened with 'Kalinka' and 'Moscow Nights', and included many famous soldiers' songs of the Great Patriotic War.

(**Right**) NKVD sleeve patch, early 1940s; in outline this represents the sword and shield motif. In the 1930s-40s NKVD badges were worked on a cloth background of their traditional brick-red colour; when it was attached to the uniform – on both upper sleeves – the cloth was cut down to an oval following the shape of the shield.

Although sleeve patches had a long career in the Red Army, in World War II they were the rare distinctive sign of élite units or personnel – which included NKVD officers and political commissars.

(Above) Sleeve patches of an Air Force pilot, and a balloon observer. The USSR continued to use manned balloons for local reconnaissance until at least 1944 – conventional tethered barrage balloons were rigged to lift a small basket for one or two men. The danger of this archaic procedure in the early years of complete German air superiority can hardly be overstated.

The VVS sleeve patches worn in World War II had been introduced as early as 1924: crossed swords on a winged propeller for pilots, anchored wings for balloon observers, and crossed tools for techicians and mechanics. The patches came on variously coloured bases to match the uniforms – e.g. dark blue for parade dress, white for summer parade, grey for winter coats. The patches were cut down to a wide variety of shapes (three versions can be seen in one photograph in **SUM**, page 22); individuals cut and sewed on the patches for themselves. The Air Force patches were officially discontinued under the 1943 uniform regulations, but some pilots continued to display them.

(Right) Sergeant first class, Red Air Force, 1941. This rank was introduced in 1940, replacing the previous 'squad leader', with the same collar insignia of two red-enamelled triangles in front of the branch badge on the pale blue patch. The VVS sleeve patch was worn on the left upper arm by all qualified ranks, not only officers. Note also the parachute qualification badge on his left breast. The use of such parachute jump badges dated back to the early 1930s.

(**Opposite below, & above**) *Anti-tank artillerymen, 1944. Just visible on the upper left arms of the enlisted men is the only wartime sleeve patch awarded to a Red Army ground forces branch. The patch (right) was a horizontal black diamond, piped in scarlet, and bearing either a brass artillery collar patch badge, or the crossed cannons simply painted in yellow to the same size. This insignia was a sign of the high prestige of anti-tank gunners, who took great risks; they were expected to keep firing until overrun by the Panzers, and even after the introduction of heavy 76.2mm weapons it was calculated that one AT gun and its crew would be lost for every two or three tanks knocked out – with the early 45mm guns the price was usually one for one. The badge was also unique in that it was the only Red Army sleeve patch used on field uniform in combat. It became a tradition during the war that it was displayed only by enlisted men; note in the group* **above** *that the two officers visible at left centre and right have bare sleeves.*

The weapon in both these photographs is the M1942 ZiS-3 76.2mm, not a specially designed AT gun but the standard divisional field artillery piece during the second half of the war. Its long barrel, relatively light tubular carriage, and use of the same armour-piercing round as the gun in the T-34/76 tank made it much more effective in the AT role than the field guns of other armies. The steel gun-shield was often removed, sacrificing protection for easier movement.

In the photograph **above**, *the crew from a Guards unit are posed cleaning their small arms and breech block under supervision by two officers. At left, note the Degtyarev 7.62mm DP light machine gun with its large dish magazine; at far right foreground, a Sudayev PPS-43 sub-machine gun – and a more or less waterproof German MG ammunition box being used for storing tools.*

POLITICAL OFFICERS

(Left) Red Army commissar, c.1941. This officer has the rank of political adviser (politruk), equivalent to senior lieutenant, used for political personnel from 1935. Neither the line officers' branch-of-service badge on the collar patches, nor the rank chevrons in red and gold worn on both forearms under the December 1935 regulations, were ever worn by political officers. They did, however, wear appropriately coloured branch collar patches – in this case probably rifles. The political officer's red star insignia is just visible here on both forearms of the gymnastiorka; the shirt-tunic is of rather old-fashioned appearance, with concealed buttons and patch breast pockets set on at an inward slant. His M1931 field belt is identified by the officer's whistle in its pocket on the left shoulder brace. Just visible at the bottom of the original print are the padded lines of a pair of paler khaki winter over-trousers, a sure sign of front line service.

(Right) Pair of forearm insignia for political officers, here still uncut from their factory backing. The commissars who wore them faced summary execution if they fell into German hands. From 1942 the former system of dual command – with a politruk holding equal authority with the line commander of his unit – was discontinued, and thereafter the commissar was subordinated to the combat officer (though still having considerable influence). This was one lesson learned from the disastrous defeats of summer 1941.

(Left) Reverse of the commissar's insignia. To avoid misuse of this badge, which conferred immediate authority on its wearer, the large sheets of uncut patches were carefully stamped with various detailed information, numbered and signed.

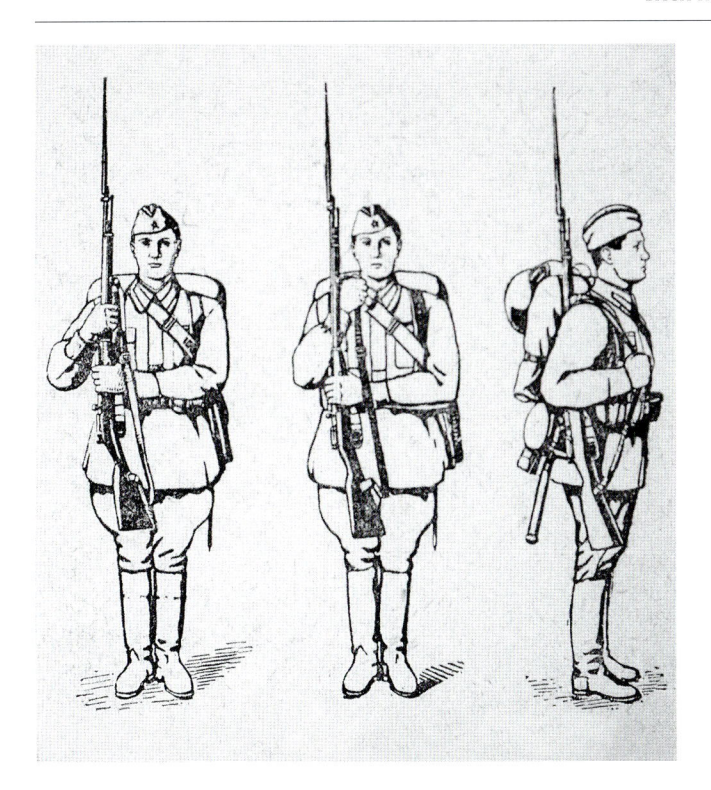

(**Left & above**) Drill positions, and bayonet fighting technique, from the 1941 infantry manual. The idealised soldier illustrated here has the M1936 helmet with a painted red star. The personal equipment is complete as per regulations, including an entrenching tool and canteen on his right hip, a bag for the BN gasmask on his left, and a knapsack with its support straps attached at the front to his belt ammunition pouches, and a greatcoat rolled and secured around it. Such completeness is seldom seen in front line photos; the entrenching tool, in particular, was rarely issued.

(**Below left**) The M1938 canvas knapsack, here with the rain cape/tent section rolled beneath it rather than around it as in the manual drawings, and with an aluminium canteen/messtin combination attached.

(**Below**) Far more common throughout the war was the simple bag-like canvas veshchevoi meshok pack. Most wartime examples of the 'veshmeshok' lacked the external buttoning pocket, and had the external stowage straps for the greatcoat, tent section and spare boots cut away.

FIELD KITCHENS

(Right) Field cook, 1944. The usual Red Army field uniform of gymnastiorka, breeches and boots is simply completed with a white cap and apron. Since the former is a working rather than a uniform headgear it does not bear a badge. The uniform is without any badges or piping; since they had no distinctive colour or emblems, field cooks and bakers usually wore the insignia of the units to which they were attached. Cooks and bakers were, however, awarded Excellent Cook and Excellent Baker badges from 1942 (see page 42 for representative appearance of Excellence badges). The design of the former included a truck-drawn field kitchen, but the reality in the field was usually less elaborate, and the wartime photograph on the opposite page provides a more typical scene.

This cook is shown inside a commandeered building or bunker occupied by senior command personnel. The machinery on the floor at left is an air filtration apparatus in case of gas attack; such high security equipment was seen only in major headquarters, to safeguard senior commanders.

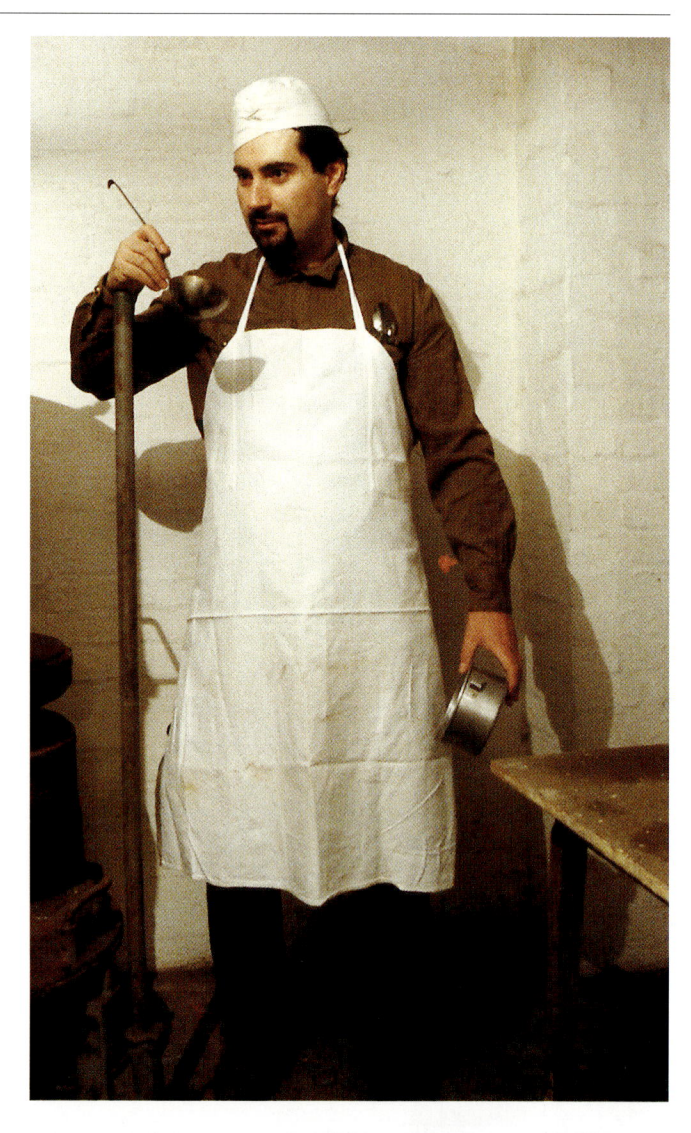

(Below) Troops line up at a horse-drawn field kitchen some time in 1943–45. The lack of common clothing and equipment is striking. Half of them have puttees and ankle boots rather than high boots, and one has a sewn canvas belt rather than leather. These expedients, together with pocketless shirt-tunics, were common even among junior officers in the later war period. Each of these men also has a different type of messtin. Overall, their appearance recalls World War I or the Russo-Japanese War rather than a modern mid-20th century army.

(**Left**) *Nazi propaganda leaflet exhorting Soviet troops to surrender; the Russian headline read 'Soldiers, the soup is ready!' Instead of ideological arguments, the text simply claims that Soviet prisoners of war will enjoy better treatment and better food in German prison camps than they do in the ranks of the Red Army. (Considering the huge numbers of Soviet prisoners who were simply allowed to starve to death in captivity, this is a particularly repulsive promise.) Food as a propaganda weapon was used also by the Red Army in the liberated territories.*

(**Below**) *At squad level the soldiers usually improvised their cooking arrangements over campfires, using locally salvaged or confiscated utensils and ingredients. Note the German jerrycan that the guitarist is using as a seat. Troops often fished when circumstances allowed, and most Russians have always been keen gatherers of wild mushrooms. There are stories of Red Army men, too impatient to pick fruit, simply cutting down a whole fruit tree and dragging it into camp.*

MINE-CLEARING, 1943

(Opposite) Mine clearance engineers worked in teams. The operator swept the ground back and forth with an electro-magnetic detector, while the others kept behind him, ready to mark and/or probe the site of any suspicious returns picked up by the operator's earphones. The detector operator wears an older-style collarless padded winter jacket, and a pilotka cap of winter-weight woollen cloth – the earphones could not be worn comfortably with a steel helmet. In World War II today's special protective armour for ordnance disposal personnel was unknown. (One kind of metal-reinforced protective vest was used in small numbers by the Red Army during World War II, but mostly by reconnaissance troops.)

Mines posed one of the greatest dangers to the advancing troops. For some years after the war they remained a great hazard, hampering the return to normal civilian life and agriculture in the USSR and the fought-over nations of Eastern and Central Europe, where uncountable millions of mines – together with bombs, artillery and infantry munitions – lay lost and disregarded. Even 60 years after VE-Day such explosive ordnance still comes to light frequently, unearthed on construction and roadwork sites, in lakes and streams, or simply found lying scattered in woodlands. (During the Communist era in Hungary and other socialist countries, most of the discovered bombs mentioned in the news were reported to be American-made. Given the political changes that have taken place since 1989, somehow increasing numbers of Soviet munitions are reported being found, and the frequency of discovery of American bombs has steadily declined...)

(Above) Glass water canteens. Since metal canteens were not available in sufficient quantities due to the conflicting demands on strategic materials, glass substitutes were introduced in large numbers and several patterns. The various colours were due to chemicals added to the process; these made the glass stronger, and also gave it a lower melting temperature for ease of production.

(Right) The Soviet soldier's 'eating irons' were usually limited to a spoon and an all-purpose knife. Spoons, bayonets and knives were often carried in the handiest place – tucked into the top of the boot. Some soldiers also followed an old peasant custom of carving their own spoons from wood.

MINE CLEARING, 1943

MINE CLEARING, 1943

(**Right**) *The detector, with the satchel for its wooden box containing the battery-powered oscillator and telephone amplifier; and a close-up of its hand controls and earphones. The shaft was assembled from three equal lengths of wood with metal collars. The principle of the mine detector was common to all similar Allied equipments, of which the first was devised by a Polish officer in Britain in 1941. It incorporated two electrical coils, one attached to an oscillator transmitting an oscillating current of audible frequency, and the other connected to a telephone receiver. When the head of the detector was passed 3–4in above the ground, any buried metal object disturbed the current between the two coils and an audible signal was heard through the earphones.*

(**Left**) *Once the operator has located a suspicious signal, one of his team either marks it with a stake for later investigation, or probes carefully with a bayonet at a 45-degree angle, to confirm the shape and size of what he has found. He may lift and neutralise the mine himself, after patiently feeling around it to detect any wires connecting it to a booby-trap charge.*

At the beginning of the war the most common German anti-personnel mine was the S-Mine 35; its cylindrical metal case incorporated both a propellant charge – which threw it up about 3ft above the ground when the pressure- or pull-igniters were set off by an unwary foot – and a bursting charge surrounded by about 360 large ball bearings. By the time the Red Army was making its great advances in 1943–45 a number of virtually non-metallic mines had been devised, to foil electronic detection. In 1942 the first model of Schü-Mine *appeared, a lethally simple invention with a wooden box case; in 1943 it was joined by the* Glas-Mine, *of which the heavy glass casing also provided a shrapnel effect, and other types were made from bakelite or ceramics.*

Captured Czech-made Mauser bayonets were favoured for probing, since they had the longest blades of any type of knife-bayonet available on the Eastern Front. In practice, relatively few electrical mine detectors were available, and the great majority of primary detection – especially by infantry, for anti-personnel mines – had to be carried out by probing. This was time-consuming under even the best circumstances, and if the minefield was properly protected by enemy observation and fire it was more or less impossible by daylight. Under battle conditions soldiers of all the combatant armies took enormous risks in order to keep up the momentum of an attack.

(**Below**) *Perhaps the last Red Army graffiti surviving from the war, on a wall in a small Hungarian town, records mine clearance: 'No mines – 7 November 1944'.*

(Opposite) The crew of a 37mm M1939 automatic anti-aircraft cannon in 1943. Despite the risky lack of a gunshield for the crew, this weapon was often pressed into service against ground targets; an experienced crew could load and fire its five-round clips at a rate of up to 80 rounds per minute. The white patch and red star painted at the base of the barrel presumably marks a destroyed enemy aircraft or vehicle; although logically one would expect a swastika or cross, VVS air aces also marked their victory tallies with red stars. Note that all the M1940 helmets here have daubs of camouflage paint added to the original olive surface.

(Opposite below) The nerve centre of a unit, 1944. Apart from one captain, right, all the soldiers manning the communications in this field headquarters are enlisted ranks. A field telephone exchange has been attached to the wall of the timber house (left background); the man at left foreground is operating a teletype machine, and the one at far right a field radio – quite a novelty at this level. The men in the centre are collating the information received and adding it to maps.

(Above) The Soviet forces used a variety of slightly differing versions of the *telogreika* cotton-padded winter jacket (and matching over-trousers) throughout the war years. The usual collarless type, first introduced in 1931, had no place to display collar patches of branch and rank. In 1943 this fall-collar type began to appear, with various buttoning arrangements at the front and cuffs. After the **Prikaz 25** uniform reforms of 15 January 1943 restored the shoulder boards, these were sometimes attached even to the padded jacket; in this case they are the plain olive field type, piped in rifles red and with the three transverse bars of a sergeant. The padded jacket originated as folk clothing in China, Mongolia and Central Asia.

(Right) Enlisted ranks' trousers – more properly, breeches. Characteristics of wartime manufacture were wide, loose thighs, and pressed metal buttons. There were no belt loops; these early trousers were either secured with braces (suspenders), or simply fastened at the back. They were made from woollen cloth for temperate and cold seasons, and sometimes from a pale khaki lightweight material for summer use. Although it is sometimes seen in wartime photographs (e.g. page 35 top), the diamond-shaped doubled reinforcement on the knees, often found on trousers described as of wartime manufacture, did not in fact become common until well after the war. Officers' breeches often bore branch-colour seam piping.

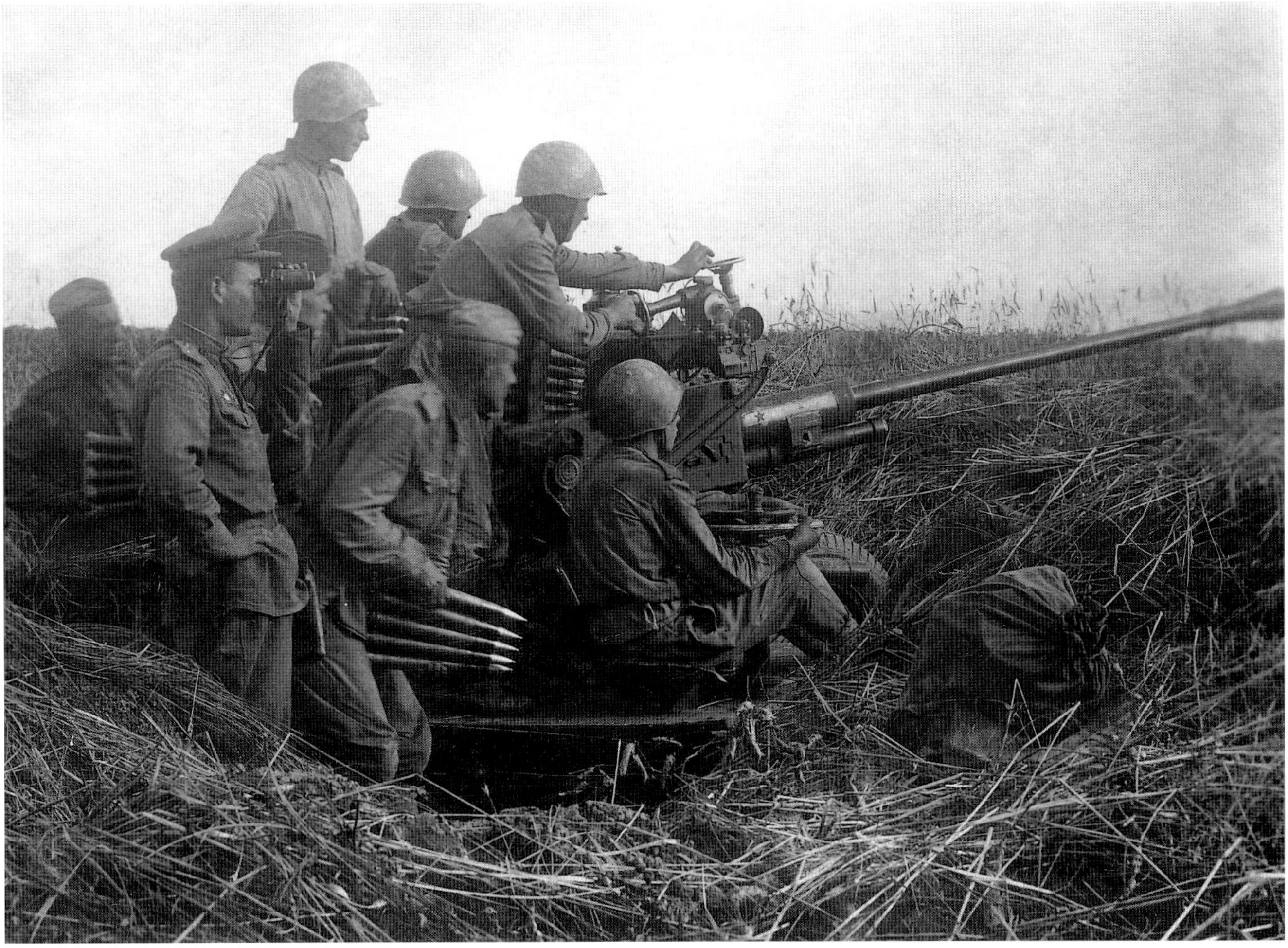

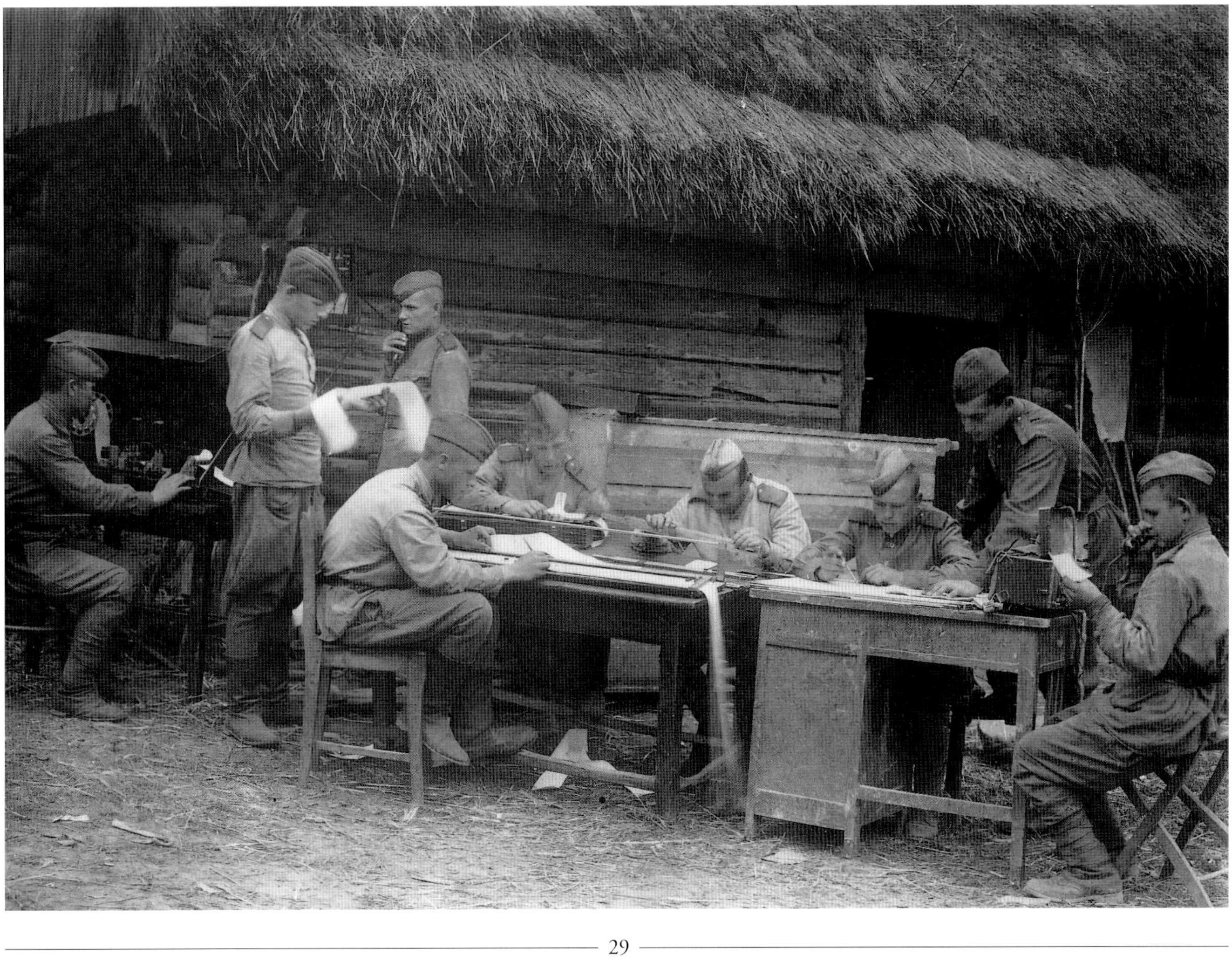

WOMEN'S ROLES IN THE GREAT PATRIOTIC WAR

It can be stated with confidence that the sacrifices faced by the women of the Soviet Union were the greatest of any among the combatant nations. The aspirations of the Soviet state towards modernity were partly based on abolishing the social gap between the sexes. Women were offered equal access to careers not only in education, the sciences and the arts, but also in heavy industry, transport and agriculture. In 1941–45 their various contributions to the war effort became increasingly vital; their sex did nothing to shelter them from its inevitable hardships and dangers, or from the harsh demands of a totalitarian state defending the very life of the nation. Women freed men for the fighting services by taking their places in the fields and factories, the telecommunications and postal services, the transport network, and in all kinds of home defence, from digging anti-tank ditches to manning anti-aircraft batteries.

The scale of casualties suffered by the USSR, both in the armed services and in the civilian populations exposed to total warfare and an enemy occupation of often medieval brutality, were staggering. Even early estimates arrived at a total of some 20 million dead, perhaps one-third of them civilians. There were mothers who lost as many as nine children on various battlefields.

Women were also involved in conventional military service. The USSR was a pioneer in the commitment of women to the same military duties as many of their menfolk. In all the wartime armies women in uniform served in the administrative, medical, communications, logistics and other non-combatant departments; but only in the Soviet Union did they serve in combat, not only as partisans (of whom an estimated 27,000 were women), but as regular troops. Some 800,000 women served, three-quarters of them conscripts; anti-aircraft defence accounted for some 300,000 of these, but they also included machine-gunners, snipers, members of reconnaissance units, combat aircrews and tank crews, as well as front-line medics (of which they made up more than 40 per cent). They were honoured with the same medals and awards as the men, and suffered the same levels of casualties.

(Below) 'The Three Graces' – a postcard of 1943, depicting three young women anti-aircraft auxiliaries on duty at Mars Field, a large park in Leningrad; the Neva bridge is just visible at the top between the AA guns. They wear greatcoats – probably the standard male version – with newly issued M1943 collar patches and shoulder boards. Although this M1936 helmet was issued in large numbers early in the war, by 1943 it had been almost entirely replaced in combat units by the M1940. However, it was still issued to second-line personnel such as these; and in besieged Leningrad up-dating the garrison's helmets would have a very low priority, given the tenuous lines of supply.

(**Opposite & right**) *Awards for raising children were introduced during World War II. The 'Glory of Motherhood Order' in three classes (opposite), and the Motherhood Medal in gold and silver classes (right), were instituted in July 1944 and first awarded that autumn. Mothers with five children received the silver medal; six, the gold medal; seven, the 3rd Class Order; eight, the 2nd Class; and nine, the 1st Class. The title 'Hero Mother' was awarded to those raising or adopting more children; the first recipient had 12 children, and another family adopted 48 war orphans.*

(**Left**) *This portrait of a captain of the Army administrative service in 1945 leaves no doubt that whatever her nominal duties, she had seen extensive service in the front lines. The three medals on her left breast include two city defence or liberation medals – probably those for 'Defence of Moscow' and 'Liberation of Vienna', to judge by the patterns of the ribbons. Two awards of the Order of the Red Star are pinned to her right breast; this was most commonly awarded for serious wounds. Below these is the Guards badge. Guard status was granted to units from September 1941, and the badge was established in March 1942, for long periods of distinguished combat service. Note that she has a male officer's gymnastiorka – the female version buttoned from the other side, from right to left. In wartime it was common to see women using the male garment, which was more easily available, although in later years it was no longer tolerated.*

The photograph was taken immediately after the war, so the captain had probably returned from a front line combat unit to an office job. These narrower shoulder boards were most commonly used by legal, medical and veterinary staff; here they are in full colour with silver lace, for 'everyday' uniform. (It must be remembered that the term 'everyday' dated from the time when this referred to smart service dress; in the Soviet context it meant items for parade and walking-out uniforms, not field or working dress.) For details of the different styles of shoulder board, see pages 85–87.

(Incidentally, a final note on women's decorations: since Leonid Brezhnev notoriously had himself decorated with vast numbers of awards, a Russian joke of the 1980s claimed that the only ones he had not managed to get were 'Hero Mother' and 'Hero Town'.)

WINTER CAMOUFLAGE CLOTHING

(Right & below) This krasno-armeyets – 'Red Army man' – in either the Finnish winter campaign, 1939/40, or the first winter of the Great Patriotic War, 1941/42 – wears a one-piece snow camouflage coat. Of lightweight material, it is for concealment only, and gives no protection. It is loosely cut, with simple tape ties, and a capacious hood, so that it can be worn easily over his M1936 (SSh-36) helmet, greatcoat and personal equipment. He has not yet received a proper pair of winter gloves. Nevertheless, he is better prepared for winter fighting than his German enemies, who did not receive issue snow camouflage clothing – or padded jackets and trousers – until the second winter of their Russian campaign.

The use of white clothing breaks up a man's outline usefully, but does not of itself guarantee good concealment against snow, and circumstances and fieldcraft also play a large part. The strength and angle of the light are critical in either concealing or revealing a man against even an unbroken snowy background. Obviously, he becomes visible if he moves when silhouetted against dark evergreen forest; and on open ground slanting light can create revealing shadows in foot tracks from quite a distance, pointing to his possible position even if he is lying down.

(*Above & left*) The later two-piece snow camouflage suit, with a pullover hooded smock and separate overtrousers. Like the first type, it is fastened with tapes, and now has a horizontal tape for securing the hood round the helmet. Since winter mittens with separate thumb and trigger-finger were issued in large numbers for the second winter of the campaign, 1942–43, this smock has matching over-mittens attached at the cuffs. Although these improved concealment, some soldiers cut them off: they were awkward when reloading a weapon, and quickly became dirty.

The two-piece suit was usually carried rolled up in a small bag of the same material inside the backpack, or in the gasmask satchel.

(**Above**) Advancing troops, including reconnaissance personnel, examine some kind of German ordnance. At bottom left, note the over-trousers in camouflage pattern worn by the senior lieutenant. This is one of surprisingly few known photographs showing the camouflage suit in the front lines. Many photographs have been published, but the great majority of these – especially those of women snipers – were posed for propaganda purposes far from the fighting.

The summer camouflage clothing came in both a one-piece overall and a two-piece suit. The latter was of the same cut as the snow camouflage version. The so-called 'amoeba' or 'jigsaw' pattern was produced in various shades of dark green and brown over a khaki background.

(**Below**) Camouflaged artillery position, 1944. The howitzer itself is painted in a three-colour camouflage pattern, and the emplacement is covered with a net and cut grass. This venerable 152mm M1910/30 field howitzer, updated with rubber tyres in 1930, was still in use at the end of the war.

(*Above*) Construction and camouflage lecture, early 1944: Red Army senior NCOs and officers learn how to build and camouflage bunkers. Priority was always given to such subjects – indeed, although they had disappeared by 1941, back in 1922 camouflage engineers and troops had their own collar patch device. The sitting sergeant has double-knee breeches; this kind of extra reinforcement at the knees became common only in the 1950s. Hanging on the wall above the instructional models are a white and two summer camouflage smocks, the patterned type on the left and on the right the plain khaki version which had bunches of string all over its surface for attaching foliage.

(*Left*) Total camouflage, summer 1944: a 45mm anti-tank gun is completely hidden with crops or long grass. These soldiers all have their pilotka caps turned back to front to avoid reflections off the red star badge – and to avoid comrades behind them mistaking a faded pilotka for a German Feldmütze.

(**Above**) *Camouflage on the move, 1944. The air support available to the advancing Red Army was largely limited to tactical types such as the Il-2 Stormovik, so they relied on moving heavy artillery forward. This 152mm weapon, being towed by a Stalinets tractor, is thoroughly camouflaged, apparently with birch trees. Its double wheels with solid tyres suggest that it is a M1937 ML-20 gun-howitzer, produced in large numbers from 1937 to 1946 and the backbone of the Soviet artillery right up to the capture of Berlin.*

Note the marching soldiers, left. The infantryman in the left background has full equipment: rolled tent section/rain cape, entrenching tool, backpack and several side bags. The others are artillerymen – the crew of the gun – and carry only their small arms, the rest of their gear being stowed on the gun or the tractor.

(**Below**) *'Katyusha' 12 × 122mm rocket launchers, 1944–45 – the shrieking 'Stalin Organs'. The sheets over the front of the projector banks are simple tarpaulins, not camouflage nets. Very little is now needed – the Luftwaffe has almost been driven from the skies, and the Red Air Force fighter cover is much stronger.*

PILOTKAS

The pilotka cap was one of the most universal features of Red Army uniform in World War II (and for long afterwards). Its popular name – 'cap for pilots' – dated from the first two decades of the century, and it was originally worn, with a strange chinstrap in a raised position, by aircrew and cadets. It cannot properly be called a summer cap, since due to the lack of a proper alternative in the early part of the war it was often worn in winter as well. This became so common that winter versions were expressly made in heavy woollen cloth (see overleaf).

This series of caps are (above, from left to right):

(1) Tank troops, in steel-grey, with black star badge backing and officer's red piping. From 1935 the élite armoured branch had the privilege of wearing regulation uniforms in grey rather than khaki, with matching headgear.

The officer's pilotka, with piping and badge backings in branch colours, was introduced throughout the Red Army in 1935; (1) to (3) here have had the usual red-enamelled brass star badge removed for photography, to show the normally almost hidden badge backings – a miniature version of those long seen on the budionovka.

(2) Red Army officer's cap, with scarlet piping and badge backing (see also right). This was general issue, the red being worn not as a branch colour but reflecting the regulation scarlet collar and cuff piping of the M1935 officer's gymnastiorka.

(3) Air Force officer's cap, in dark blue with pale blue piping and badge backing. Although it remained an integral part of the Red Army, and continued to wear khaki working and flying dress, the Air Force (Voyenno-Vozdushnye Sily) received a dark blue dress uniform in 1924.

In the second half of the war these colourful caps were hardly used. Officers preferred field quality visored caps, or simply wore the same plain khaki pilotka as their men.

(4) A summer version of the ordinary soldiers' pilotka, in lightweight pale sand-khaki cloth, here with the standard cap badge without cloth backing.

PILOTKAS

(Above) A hasty all-arms officers' conference in the field, summer 1944. Note the variety of field headgear: pilot's leather flying helmet (left foreground); field quality khaki cap with plastic visor (second left); tank crew (or possibly, motorcyclist's) padded canvas protective helmet (middle foreground); Air Force full colour pilotka (right foreground); and two enlisted ranks' khaki pilotkas (centre & right background).

(Right & opposite) Two examples of winter-weight pilotkas. These enlisted ranks' caps were made from various shades and qualities of material, and both smaller and larger cap stars were used.

(Opposite top) A group of officers wearing field uniforms with full decorations immediately after the German surrender in spring 1945. Note that the visibility of the headgear has been reduced to the minimum. One visored cap (rear, left) is worn without a badge, and the three men at right use the enlisted ranks' plain pilotka without piping or cloth star badge backing. Note (right foreground) the old officers' belt set still worn with two shoulder braces.

38

PILOTKAS

(Above) Cap badges. Although there were regulations for the use of variously sized zhvezda – cap stars – basically the same badge was used by all ranks for the pilotka, naval bezkozirka, officers' visored cap, and winter ushanka. This selection show a variety of shapes, finishes, and sizes both of stars and hammer-and-sickle motifs. (Top centre) naval officer of a non-combatant branch – see also page 54; (centre) general officer's M1940 for winter lambskin papaha and visored cap. The generals' two-piece cap badge usually had a branch-coloured backing – e.g. Frontier Guards, green; Air Force, light blue, etc. (Bottom centre) NKVD VOHR – note crossed rifles.

39

AIR FORCE CAPS

(Left) Pilots, 1945. These two officers pose in gymnastiorkas with coloured, laced shoulder boards and full medals and orders. At left, the visored cap has very large gold-embroidered wings on the crown and wreath around the cap star; it is probably privately tailor-made. The junior lieutenant on the right has the old-style officers' dark blue pilotka with light blue piping, but lacking the classic light blue badge backing.

(Above) Pilots, 1944. All wear the full-colour 'everyday' visored cap with regulation insignia. Note that the officer in right foreground even has greatcoat collar patches attached to his leather flying coat, which is normally seen bare of shoulder boards or insignia. In right background the open-cockpit Polikarpov Po-2 biplanes strongly suggest that this is a training airfield far from the front.

(Right) Air Force officer's cap, with regulation insignia.

INFORMATION-GATHERING

(Above) Reconnaissance photographers, 1944. While the Red Army still employed several archaic but still effective reconnaissance techniques – the use of horsed cavalry, and manned observation balloons – this picture shows a more modern approach. A photography team are using either a Leica or a FED camera with a very long telephoto lens assembly, supported by a tripod. (These cameras were basically the same, the FED – named after Felix Dzerzhinsky – being produced from the 1930s under licence from Germany.) The second member of the team keeps a careful written record.

(Below) An extremely rare photograph of a Red Army sound detection team, 1944, presumably listening for vehicle engines and other tell-tale sounds of German activity. While they must presumably be in the very front line, the relative lack of concealment suggests that they can hardly be close enough to pick up voices; nevertheless, the telephone operator keeps his Mosin M1944 carbine handy. Since there is no recording machine evident, any useful noises overheard must have been transmitted immediately to an analyst by means of a field telephone link. Note that this expensive and delicate equipment is being operated by simple enlisted men. The operator on the left has knee reinforcement on his breeches.

INFORMATION-GATHERING

(Above) Signallers' insignia. The Excellent Signaller brass and enamel breast badge was awarded from 1943. Flanking it are two examples of the delicate branch insignia from M1935 collar patches and M1943 shoulder boards – one in fine condition complete with a red paint infill, and the other as recovered from the battlefield. The winged star and lightning bolts was used as the signals emblem from 1936, and was one of the rare branch symbols to remain unchanged throughout the later history of the USSR.

(Below) Dug in among the cabbage harvest in 1944, a sergeant supervises three privates using an artillery range finder between 5 and 6 metres long – originally a naval equipment, later adapted for the Army artillery. Since the distance between the eyepiece and the lenses was known, and the angle they created when focused on a target could be measured, the range could be calculated by simple geometry. Note the cords looped around this range finder, which were used for carrying it when on the move in the field.

INFORMATION-GATHERING

(Above & right) Two views of the classic binocular range finder in use. This equipment could be fixed to its tripod or to any chance-found support – in the photograph **above** it seems to be attached to a birch log. As so often, the soldiers display non-regulation uniform features. (Right) the right-hand sergeant sports stiff, full-colour everyday/parade shoulder boards with yellow transverse rank stripes and a branch-of-service emblem, instead of soft khaki field quality shoulder boards with red or raspberry stripes, as specified for combat zones.

43

INFORMATION-GATHERING

(Left) This artillery colonel displays two awards of the Order of the Red Banner, probably dating from service in the Civil War 20 years before. He is guarded, at right, by a private with a PPS-43 sub-machine gun. The field telephone is probably a captured German piece. A normal accessory for officers was a pair of 8×30 or 6×30 field binoculars (i.e. 6× or 8× magnification, 30mm diameter front lenses). Such equipment did not vary much between any of the armies of World War II.

(Right) Service binoculars. This particular pair are dated 1946, but offer a clear example of how optical items were stamped and dated. Various serial numbers (sometimes starting with the year of production), factory and Army quality control stamps were used during the war. This piece is marked, between the hammer-and-sickle and the serial number, for the Krasnogorsk factory near Moscow, whose symbol was the path of light through a prism.

ONE-MAN RANGE-FINDER, 1944

This infantry reconnaissance scout – 'razvedchik' – *uses a simplified version of the artillery optical equipment to calculate the location of an observed enemy position. He carries no pack, just the usual gasmask bag for his small kit and food. He sports the 1942 Guards badge on his right breast, and the raspberry-red everyday shoulder boards of the rifles attached to his* telogreika *padded jacket.*

Note, in this picture and the rear view overleaf, the details of the support system for the range finder on the shoulders and rear belt. This device was first used by cameramen covering the 1936 Berlin Olympic Games.

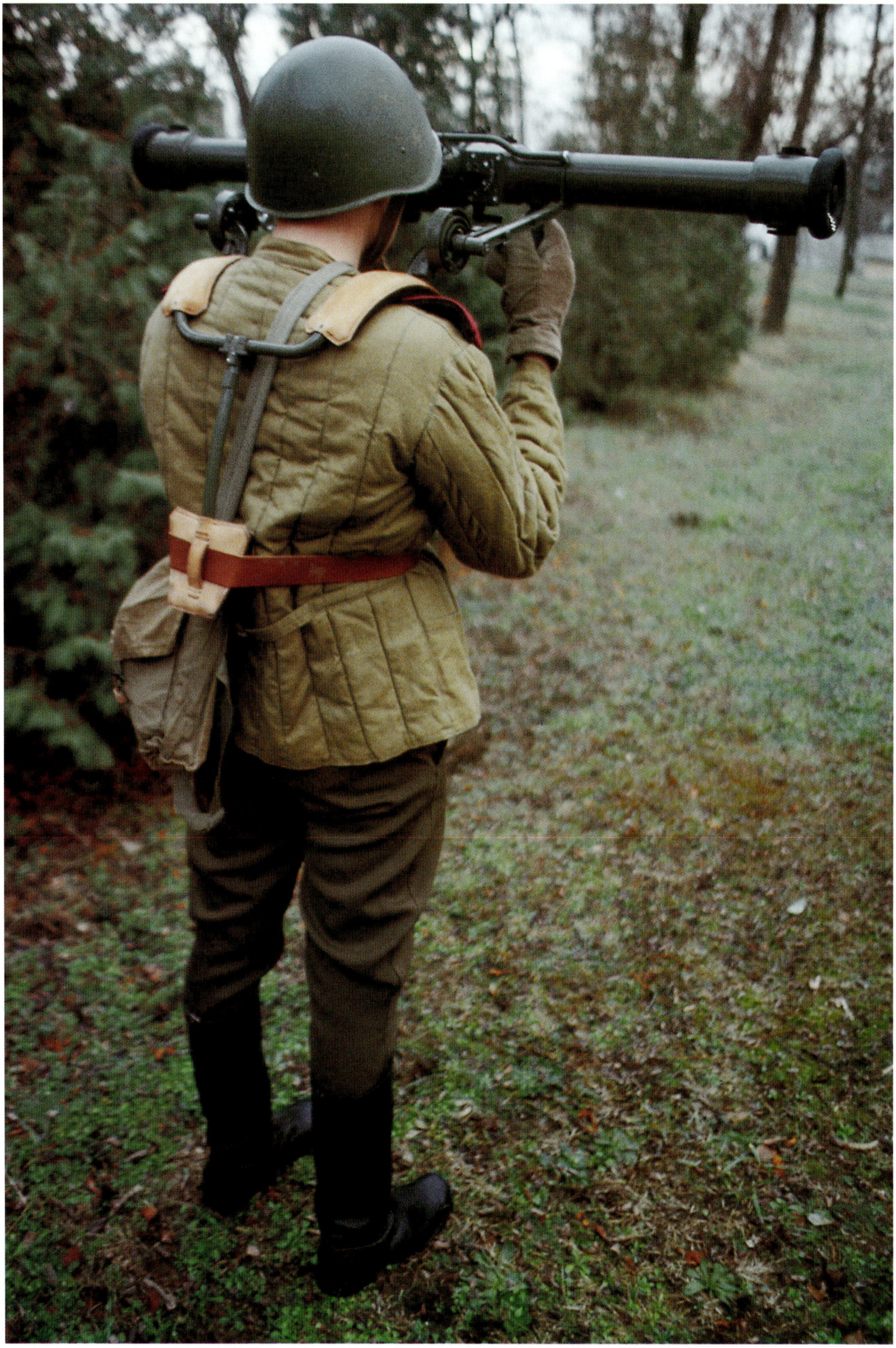

TR FIELD PERISCOPE

(*Right & below*) *This small field periscope was used by reconnaissance personnel, particularly in urban warfare zones. The slim single tube was easy to conceal, and consequently hard for the enemy to spot. The 'TR' designation was never officially explained, but may have derived from the abbreviations of* truba *and* razvedchik – *'Tube for Reconnaissance Scouts'? Like many well-proven items dating from the Great Patriotic War, it was still in use in Afghanistan 40 years later.*

Again, this scout is irregularly wearing the coloured everyday shoulder boards rather than the khaki field version. Note the M1940 helmet, with its canvas web chinstrap and low-placed fixing rivets. From the 1960s onwards four rivets were used, in a noticeably higher position – this distinguishes the SSh-68 from the SSh-40 helmet, which may be found with various different liners. Note, too, this soldier's trigger-finger mittens.

(*Opposite*) *Rear view of one-man range finder system.*

TR FIELD PERISCOPE

(Above & right) The TR was carried in a small backpack.

Note also the gasmask satchel slung on the hip. Since the Germans never used gas on the battlefields of World War II it was rare indeed to find a Soviet soldier with a gasmask in his bag. However, since the Red Army – unlike the Wehrmacht – failed to provide its troops with a Brotbeutel ('bread bag') or other general purpose haversack, the gasmask satchel was universally used for carrying food, tools, mess gear and small personal kit.

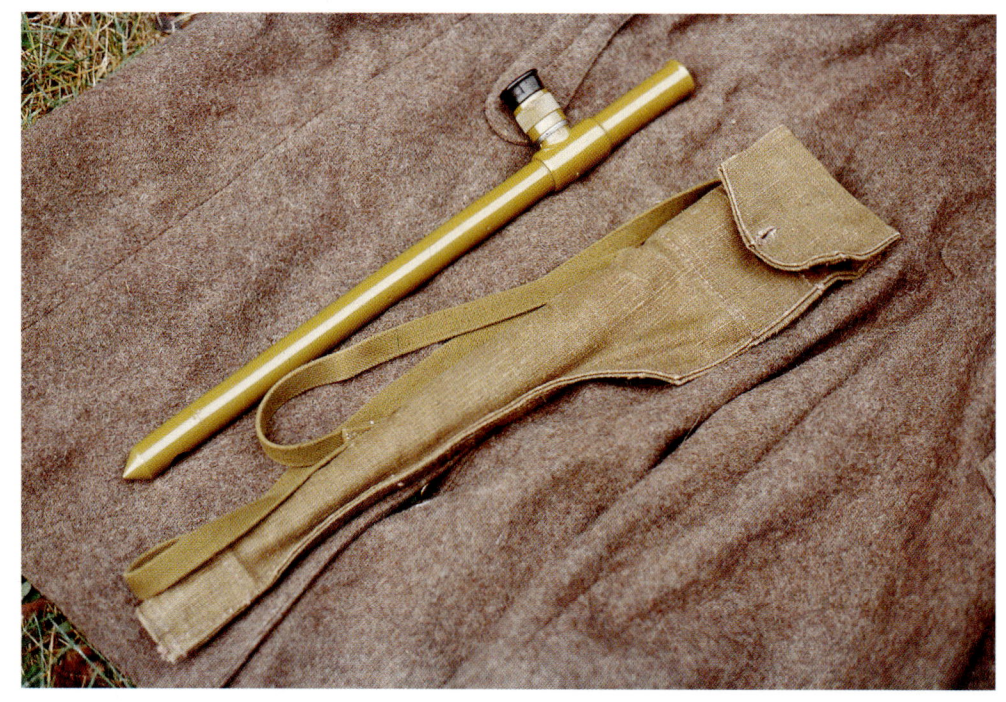

The Red Fleet

NAVAL INFANTRYMAN, NORTHERN FLEET; MURMANSK, 1942

The Soviet Union still followed an outdated strategic doctrine whereby both the Red Air Force and the Red Fleet (Navy) were subordinated to the ground forces. Apart from periods when Russia was particularly conscious of the need to project her capabilities as a modern European or global power, the Navy was relatively neglected in favour of devoting resources to mass land armies. That was the case on the eve of the Great Patriotic War; the Navy represented only five per cent of total manpower, and hundreds of thousands of naval personnel found themselves fighting as ground troops, in a tradition which echoed the temporary naval brigades of the Crimean War of the 1850s, the Russo-Japanese War of 1904–05, and World War I. In the postwar period the situation was formalised, and the Naval Infantry became a genuinely élite branch specialising in amphibious operations.

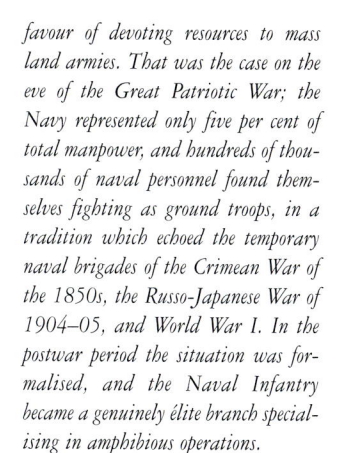

During World War II naval ground troops had mixed Navy and Army uniforms and gear, and initially suffered from lack of equipment and training for their land role. In his apparently black but actually midnight-blue 'square rig', this krasnoflotets – 'Red sailor' – is hardly distinguishable from his forerunners of 1914–17, as he guards facilities at the submarine base of the Northern Fleet, the higher command responsible for all operations north of the Baltic Sea. Since the bezkozirka sailor cap was smarter than the fleece-lined ushanka, sailors sometimes sewed warm linings inside it for winter wear. It displays white piping, the universal red star badge, a Northern Fleet cap tally, and golden-yellow anchors on the tips of the hanging ribbons. The blue-and-white striped undershirt was in all periods a proud distinctive feature of the sailor's uniforms. The short, double-breasted pea jacket or bushlat was originally used in everyday and walking-out dress, but the Navy's shortage of special winter clothing led to its being used for operations – its short length was convenient for movement. Sailors had a regulation black leather belt with a brass anchor-and-star buckle (for the Merchant Navy, without the star), but without the buckle plate for working uniform and for NCO equivalent ranks; in wartime, however, any combination of items was used as available. This sailor also wears lengths of Maxim machine gun feed belts as expedient ammunition bandoliers (empty of cartridges in our photographs). The weapon is the standard Mosin Nagant rifle, carried with the old-fashioned socket bayonet, of cruciform blade section, fixed.

NAVAL INFANTRYMAN, MURMANSK, 1942

(Left) Rear of the uniform, including the usual bell-bottomed trousers worn over shoes. Maxim belts were arranged around the waist and over either one or both shoulders. Sometimes they were even pressed into service as rifle slings, although one imagines that the brass stiffeners would quickly wear holes in the shoulders of the uniform.

(Right) The basic ammunition issue was carried in five-round clips in the belt pouches. Note that these are single-piece items, although divided internally into two compartments. Though smaller and less capacious, these pouches are not very different from the Navy's old M1898 cartridge boxes.

— 50 —

(**Left**) *A naval stoker stripped for hot work. The bezkozirka was worn at all times, even in combat; it was not until after the war that berets were introduced with working uniform. The classic bell-bottom naval trousers were worn with the blue-and-white striped undershirt, here the* maika *sleeveless version; there was also a long-sleeved* telniyashka. *In hot weather and southern areas the white naval jumper was also used without the undershirt, both for working and walking-out. The normal blue jumpers for work and combat bore numbers identifying the sailor's duty and post on board ship. A sailor still in probationary training had a number beginning with '0' and was called a 'doubler'. This meant that he was paired with an experienced hand – whose number was the same without the '0' – to show him what to do.*

(**Right**) *Naval infantryman, Black Sea Fleet, 1944. He wears the usual ground combat uniform of padded jacket and lightweight breeches with puttees, the only immediate difference being his cap and striped undershirt. His weapon is the ubiquitous PPSh-41 sub-machine gun, and he carries a canvas pouch for its 71-round drum magazine on a black naval belt, here with a silver pre-war Merchant Navy buckle. His sidearm is a poor quality M1940 'reconnaissance knife' – sometimes Tokarev rifle bayonets or captured German bayonets were also used – and he has the usual slung gasmask bag. (Courtesy Japanese Soviet Army Re-enactment Club, Tokyo)*

(Right) Naval officers, 1942. The Navy was the only military service which used standing-collar tunics continuously from Imperial times, and shoulder boards were added only after January 1943. The four cuff stripes below an embroidered star (left) mark a captain 2nd rank, and three stripes a captain 3rd rank. Before 1943 the stripes ran all the way round the cuff, but later shorter lengths were worn on the outside only, in conjunction with shoulder boards of rank. Lace, buttons, etc. were gold for sea officers and silver for technical and non-combatant branches such as medical officers.

(Below) Naval infantrymen of the Black Sea Fleet, 1945, provide a good example of Navy personnel wearing basically Red Army infantry uniform. The only naval feature displayed by the ratings is the black naval shoulder board, piped red, and bearing the yellow cypher of the Black Sea Fleet. (Khaki field shoulder boards were very rarely used by seamen.) Some career NCOs in this group wear visored caps with the enlisted ranks' field uniform. Naval infantrymen kept naval ranks, while shore-based artillery or Army-equipped technical and engineer units used Army ranks.

(Right) *Naval infantry gymnastiorka. All khaki infantry clothing and equipment issued to these units was of Red Army patterns, but occasionally small naval features were added or substituted in the field, such as the buttons on this shirt-tunic.*

(Below) *Naval infantry officers' weapons and belt, in black leather rather than the brown of the Red Army. Both the seven-shot 7.62mm Nagant M1895 revolver and the M1930 Tokarev semi-automatic of the same calibre have naval holsters, hanging below the belt on double adjustable straps. The belt section of the Nagant holster has two integral cartridge pouches. In wartime, economy versions of these leather items were made with cheaper iron fittings replacing the brass; these were therefore prone to rust.*

(Right) *Torpedo boat crew protective hood, of synthetic waterproof material; such fast coastal craft exposed their deck crews to heavy spray. This type of masked headgear was seen in several variations. Early in the war pilots had similar masks for open-cockpit aircraft, sometimes combined with goggles. Protective masks were also seen in use by flamethrower operators; and they are sometimes described as being issued to armoured train crews.*

(Below) *Naval officers' cap badges, and (bottom right) petty officers' cap badge, for visored caps. The silver version – as in the Red Army – was for officers of 'non-combatant' departments, e.g. medical, supply, construction, administrative and legal services. The oval badge with unwreathed anchor was worn by petty officers who extended their enlistments. All these badges were used on white- or black-topped visored caps; while petty officers wore the same 'square rig' as seamen, they had the distinction of officer-style caps, as well as a belt without the anchor buckle plate. Note that all these wartime badges are of fine quality gold or silver embroidery; in the postwar period they were cheaply produced from pressed metal, and only admirals had embroidered bullion badges.*

(Opposite top left) *A winter protective mask as worn by some naval and other aircrew, combined with a fleece-lined leather helmet and goggles.*

(Opposite top right) *Leather flying helmet, jacket and gloves, worn with a different model of goggles.*

(Opposite) *Naval shoulder boards and jumper tabs (top, left to right:) cadet; Baltic Fleet, for white summer shirt; Baltic Fleet, shore service and naval infantry; junior lieutenant, medical branch; major, naval aviation – this branch used Army/Air Force ranks; general or admiral, shore service and naval infantry. Seagoing admirals had an anchor embroidered in the star; note raspberry-red edging for infantry, but admirals' crossed-anchor button.*

Naval shoulder boards were introduced in early 1943; the cuff rings which had previously been the only rank insignia were retained by seagoing officers in parallel with the shoulder boards. (Bottom, left to right:) captain 1st, 2nd and 3rd rank; captain-lieutenant; lieutenant.

THE RED FLEET

(Right) *Seamen's left sleeve patches of branch or speciality, worn on the midnight-blue jumper; the yellow- or gold-ringed version was for everyday and walking-out dress orders, the plain red for working dress. In all there were some 25 patches in this range introduced from the 1930s. The last time these patches appeared in uniform regulations was during the 1950s; they were later simplified, and those of several outdated functions were discontinued.*

(Left column, top to bottom:) range finder; quartermaster, ration and material stores; boatswain.

(Centre column, top to bottom:) meteorology service; telegraphist; musician.

(Third column, top to bottom:) topman (masts & rigging); gunlayer; radio technician.

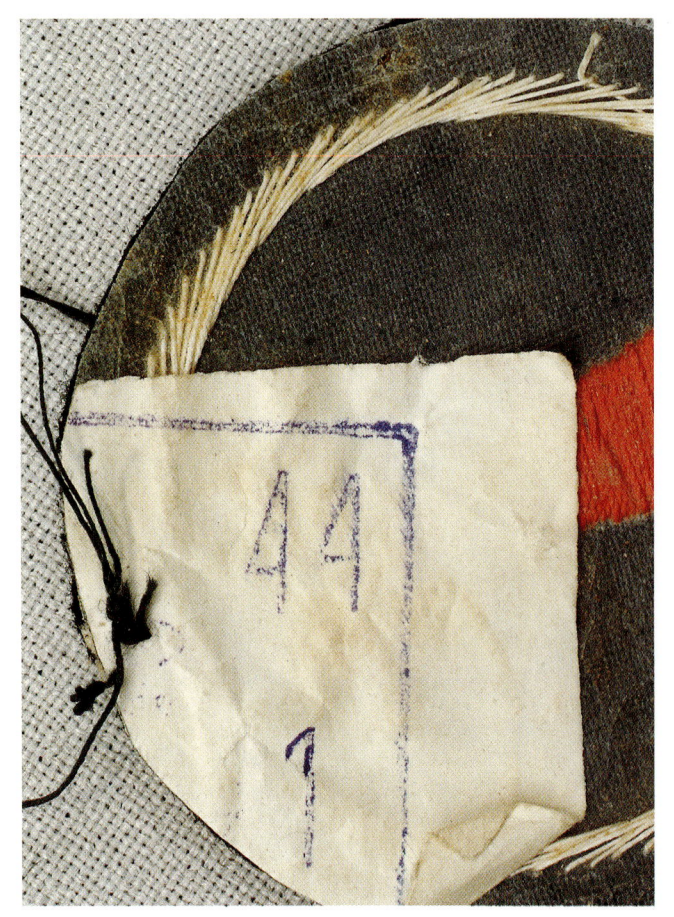

(Below) *The rear of an unused naval patch, showing a rarely seen stamped paper label dated 1944, and marked '1' for 1st class quality. Probably this single small label was applied to an entire uncut sheet or 'leaf' of about a dozen patches.*

(Below right) *Shoulder board emblem of Red Fleet seagoing engineering branch.*

Naval personnel seldom used such speciality emblems; some other exceptions were aviation, legal, medical, veterinary, shore construction and artillery branches. These others used exactly the same emblems as the Red Army – e.g. crossed cannons for artillery, crossed axes for construction, etc. The only exception was this seagoing engineers'/technicians' emblem of a boat propeller and cogged wheel. As they were a non-combatant branch the emblem was always in silver.

— 56 —

PARTISAN, 1942

Partisan warfare played an important part in the Great Patriotic War. The rapid German advances of 1941 left huge numbers of Soviet troops cut off behind the front lines, in groups numbering anything from a few stragglers to many hundreds. As time passed Moscow began to make contact with these often well-armed groups, and to harness them to the war effort. In the vast expanses of Russia, particularly in the northern forests, and the Pripet Marshes behind the Wehrmacht's Army Group Centre, the Germans had to commit many divisions of troops to hunting down partisans and securing their own lengthening lines of supply.

Partisans relied upon the support of villagers for most of their food – which was often given willingly, but sometimes taken by force. Ruthless German security troops, such as the notorious brigades of the Kommandostab Reichsführer-SS, routinely massacred entire villages suspected of contact with partisans, or simply as a warning. It is hardly surprising that some civil populations co-operated with the Germans out of fear, or the wish to protect themselves from marauding bands; it is seldom appreciated that there were also large numbers of anti-Soviet partisans, some of whom remained active for several years after 1945, particularly in the Baltic region and the Ukraine.

(Right) This partisan certificate was issued to male and female members of the Komsomol (Communist youth organisation), usually under the age of 25, for taking part in the 'Active fight against the German Invaders'.

(Above) This pro-Soviet partisan has mixed clothing. Throughout the Soviet period such boots, padded clothing and khaki sharovary breeches were commonly used not only by the Red Army but also by civilians, especially construction or forestry workers in rural regions. This man's padded telogreika is covered with a sleeveless leather jerkin of the type used by British, Canadian and US troops during their interventions early in the Civil War; it may also be a captured World War II Hungarian or Romanian issue. His M1895 Winchester rifle probably identifies him not as a member of a large ex-Red Army unit, but as an individual former hunter.

PARTISAN, 1942

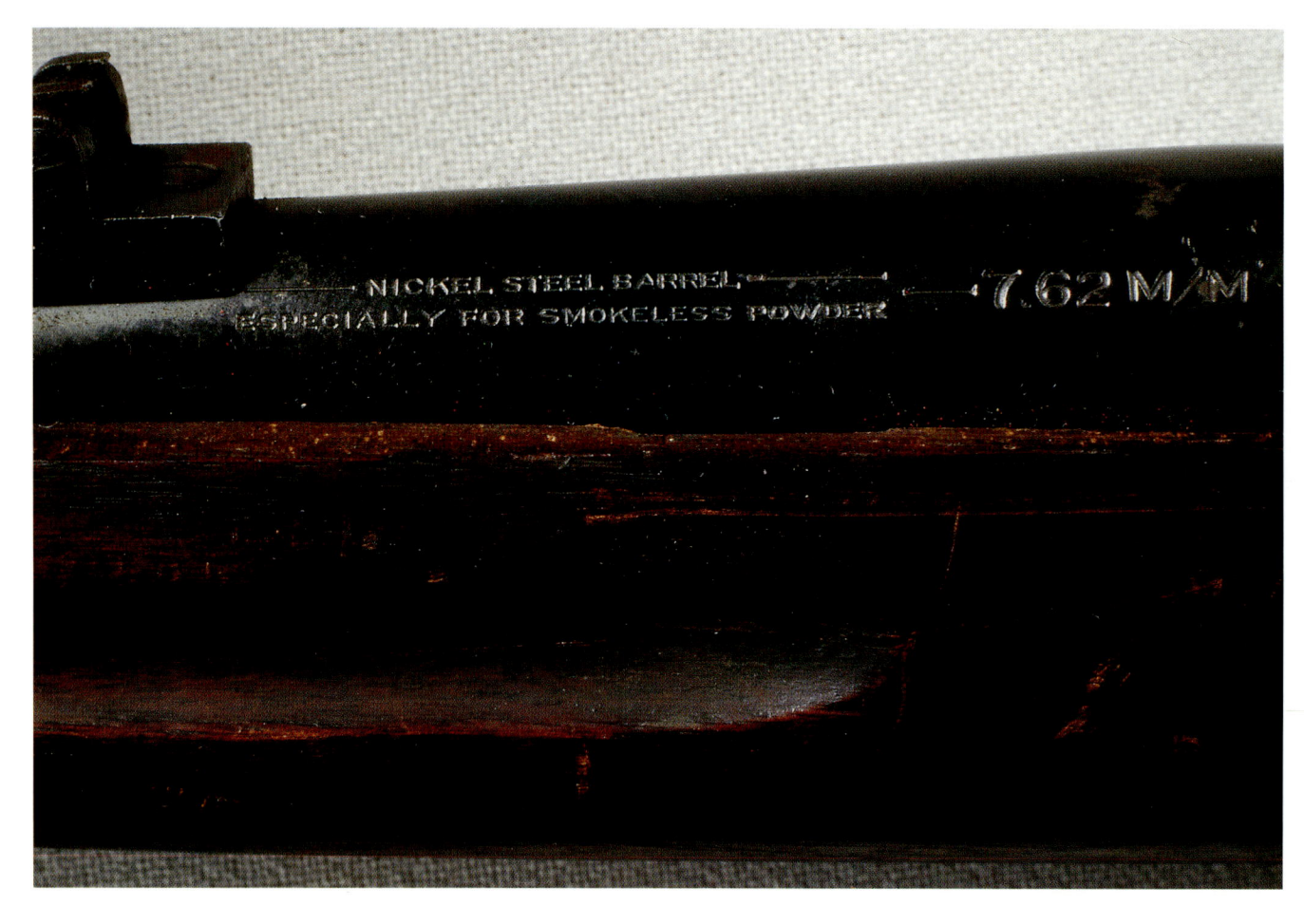

(Above & centre) In World War I, Russia ordered John Moses Browning's Winchester M1895 lever-action box-magazine repeating rifle, modified to take Russian 7.62mm ammunition that could be loaded by thumbing the rounds down from the Russian five-round stripper clip. In the Tsar's army this excellent weapon became the preferred equipment of Guard and other élite units; the Red Army inherited it, and during the Civil War large numbers fell into the hands of civilians. The Germans reported its presence on all fronts in World War II, and until quite recently it was still popular with hunters in many Eastern Bloc states. Note on the left of the barrel the inscription 'Nickel-steel barrel especially for smokeless powder'.

(Right) The left side of the action, with opened breech. It is engraved 'Manufactured by the Winchester Repeating Arms Co, New Haven, Conn, U.S.A.' above a list of patent dates from May and December 1895, August 1897, January and August 1898, to August 1907.

(Left & below) Details of the Winchester M1895 Russian. Note manufacturer's stamp, and the Imperial quality control stamp seen on all wooden and metal parts. The rifles were effective up to 1,400 metres; they took an American-made bayonet, but this was hardly seen in Russia.

The Imperial Army both imported foreign weapons and manufactured some under licence (for instance, the Nagant revolvers and rifles were originally designed by a Belgian engineer). The new Soviet regime would follow the tradition, and bought or copied technical innovations from its earliest to its final days – e.g. Swiss clock mechanisms, German Leica cameras, weapons including rocket technology, American engines, trucks, cars and aircraft all became the prototypes for Soviet products.

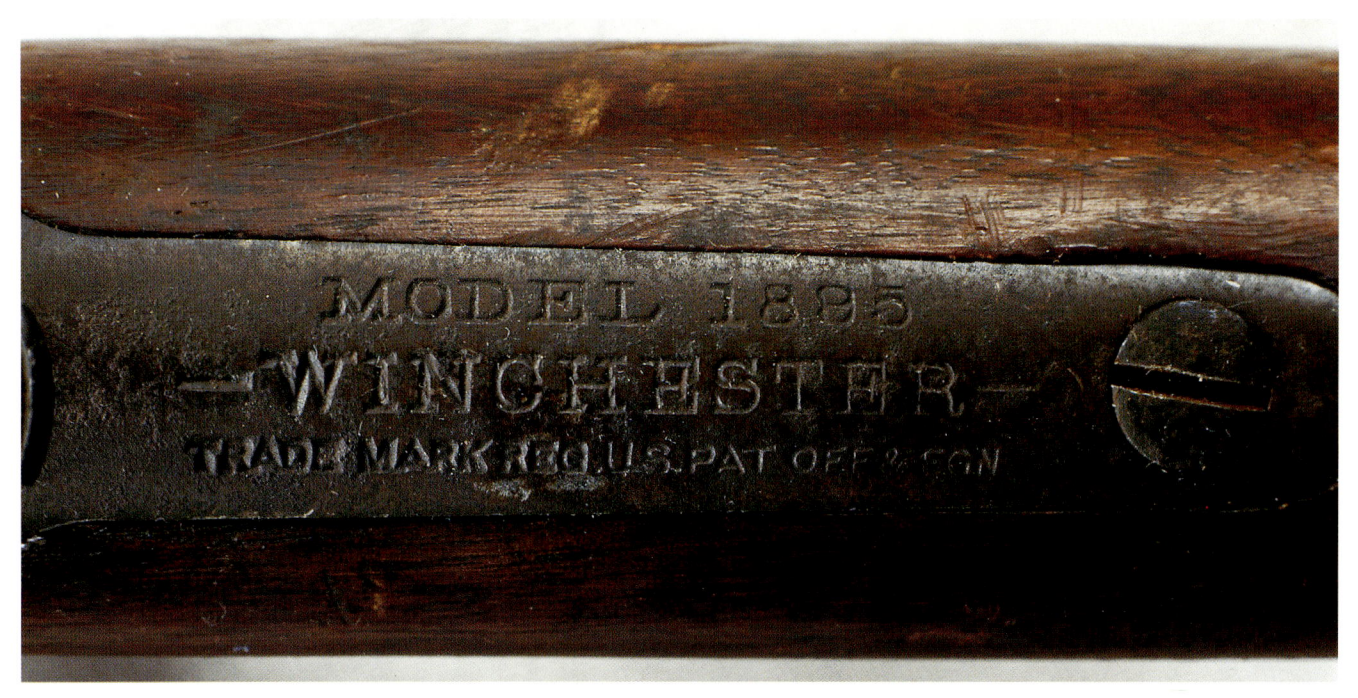

THE ANCESTOR OF MODERN SURVIVAL GUIDES

The hard-cover booklet '*Partisan's Companion*' of 1941 (the word *sputnik* means companion) describes most Soviet and German pistols, rifles, grenades, sub-machine guns, machine guns and mortars. Partisans cut off from any major sources of Soviet supply obviously had to capture the bulk of their weapons and ammunition. (Indeed, the Soviet government itself enthusiastically re-used captured matériel; the 22-ton SU-76/L42 self-propelled gun employed the chassis and running gear of German Panzer III tanks.) The *Companion* also illustrated, for instance, hand-to-hand and bayonet fighting techniques, the manufacture of 'Molotov cocktails', and recommended practices for sabotage and camouflage. It is also a true survival guide: the reader could learn how to make fire and encampments, cross rivers, read maps, give first aid and carry the wounded.

(**Top right**) *Hand-to-hand fighting with an entrenching tool. Oddly, the picture shows an enemy wearing a British (or US M1917) helmet; the booklet presumably re-used material prepared during the 1930s when the supposed enemy was Western intervention forces.*

(**Right**) *'Neutralising' a German motorcyclist.*

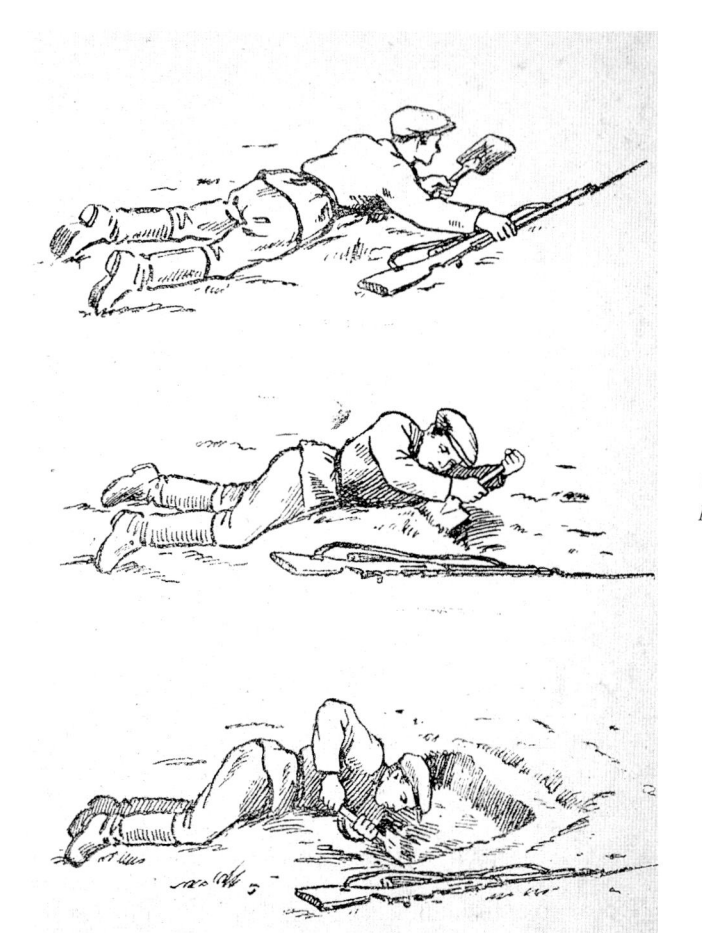

(**Left & above**) *Making a hasty rifle pit for minimal cover in action.*

THE ANCESTOR OF MODERN SURVIVAL GUIDES

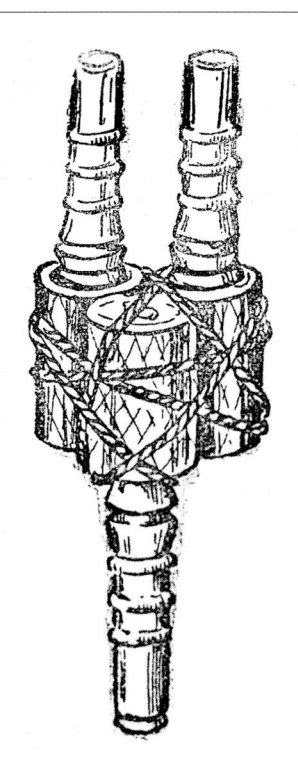

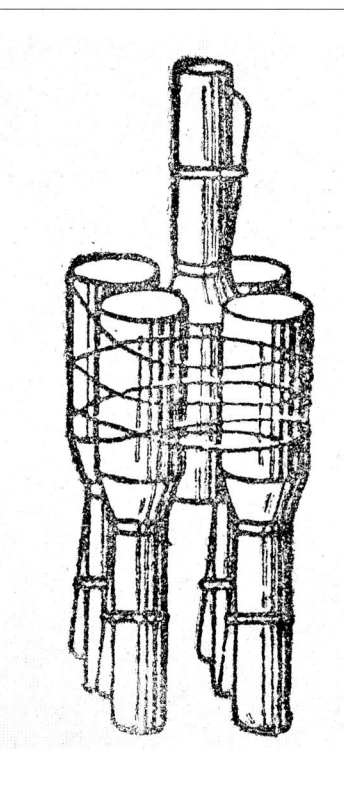

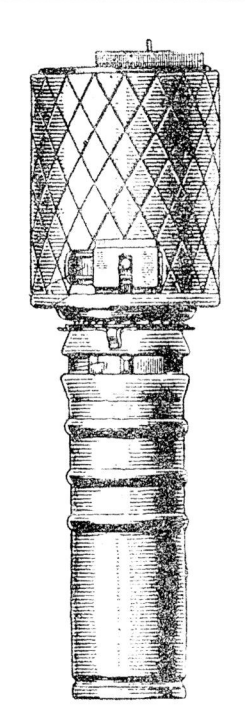

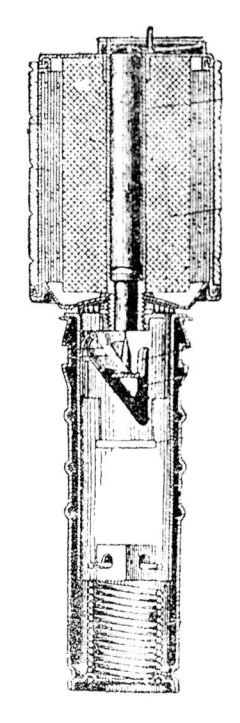

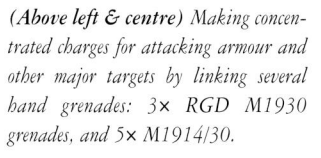

(Above left & centre) Making concentrated charges for attacking armour and other major targets by linking several hand grenades: 3× RGD M1930 grenades, and 5× M1914/30.

(Above right) Details of the M1930 grenade, with its fragmentation sleeve; and (right) arming the M1930, with its twist safety device.

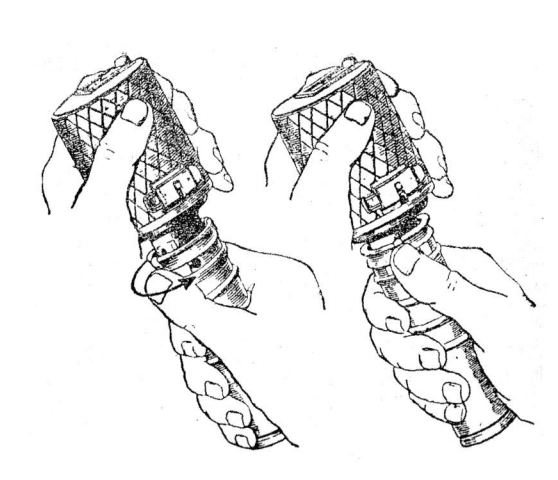

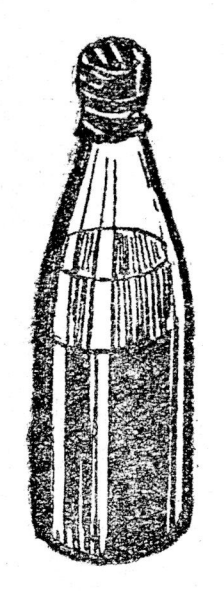

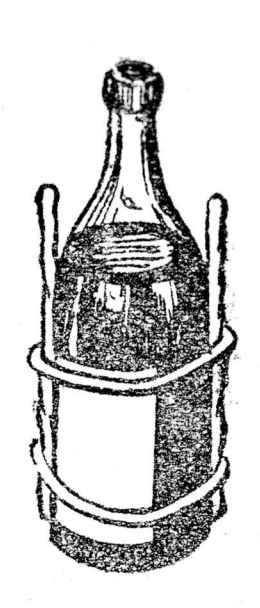

(Left) Although this expedient incendiary grenade is known world-wide as a 'Molotov cocktail', in the USSR this would have been thought disrespectful of the Soviet Foreign Minister V.I.Molotov; it was formally called butyikas goryuchej smes'yu, *'bottle with flammable mixture'*. Long after it was discarded by all but guerrillas on other fronts, the Red Army still counted it as a useful part of the infantryman's anti-tank armament. It could be made from any glass bottle, using alcoholic spirit or petrol for instant ignition, mixed with a heavy oil or tar for adhesion and longer burning. The Red Army provided some more sophisticated means of ignition than the classic spirit-soaked rag stuffed into the neck of the bottle and set alight just before throwing. 'Incendiary liquid kits' were an issue item: these included (centre) two glass tubes of sulphuric acid, coupled to the bottle with thick rubber bands, or (right) impact detonators cushioned on a piece of cotton waste.

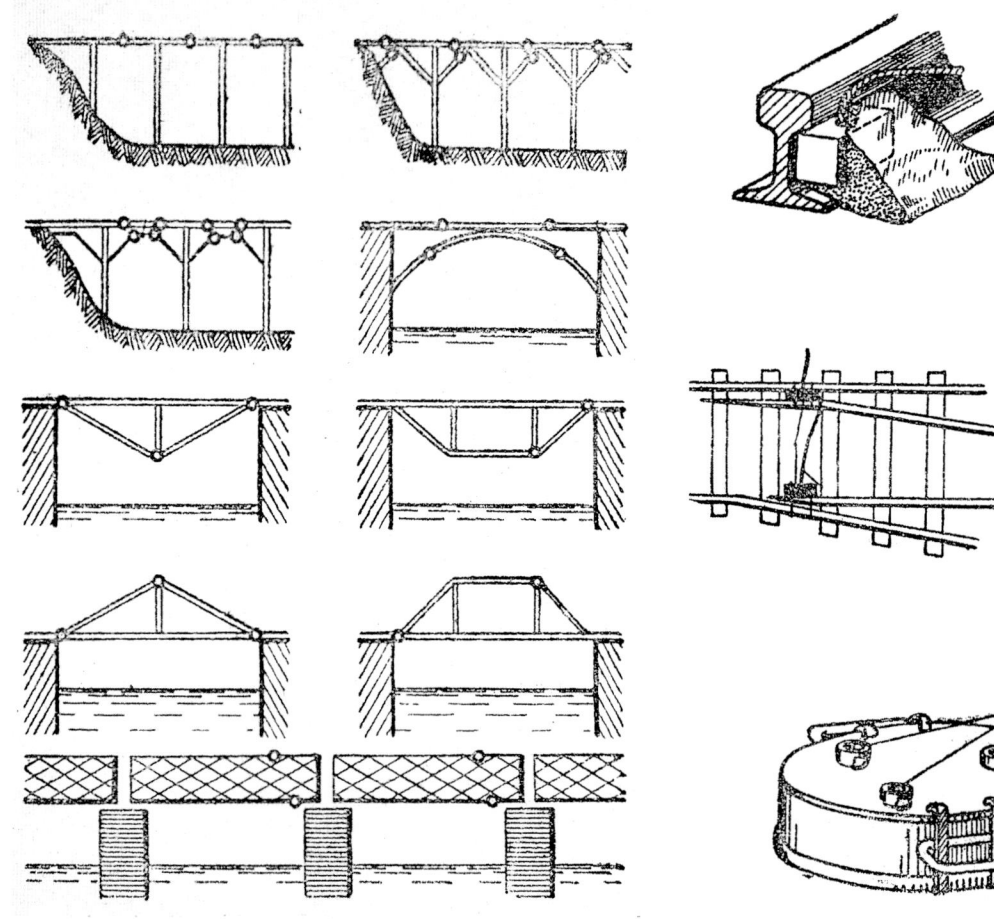

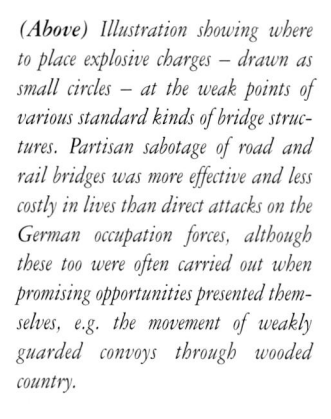

(Above) Illustration showing where to place explosive charges – drawn as small circles – at the weak points of various standard kinds of bridge structures. Partisan sabotage of road and rail bridges was more effective and less costly in lives than direct attacks on the German occupation forces, although these too were often carried out when promising opportunities presented themselves, e.g. the movement of weakly guarded convoys through wooded country.

(Above right) Methods for destroying rail tracks with explosive charges and anti-tank mines. In the huge and under-populated expanses of the USSR the news of victory in 1945 took some time to reach every corner of the country; there were legends about isolated partisans still blowing up bridges and railways long after the formal end of the war.

(Right) Several different suggestions for improvising stretchers, litters or barrows for carrying the wounded. The booklet also shows how two men can carry a casualty by a simple 'chair lift', with or without the aid of belts. The most common method of casualty evacuation was in fact lying on a tent section carried by four soldiers; if under fire, or if that many hands were not available, male and female medical orderlies were taught to drag the casualty along the ground.

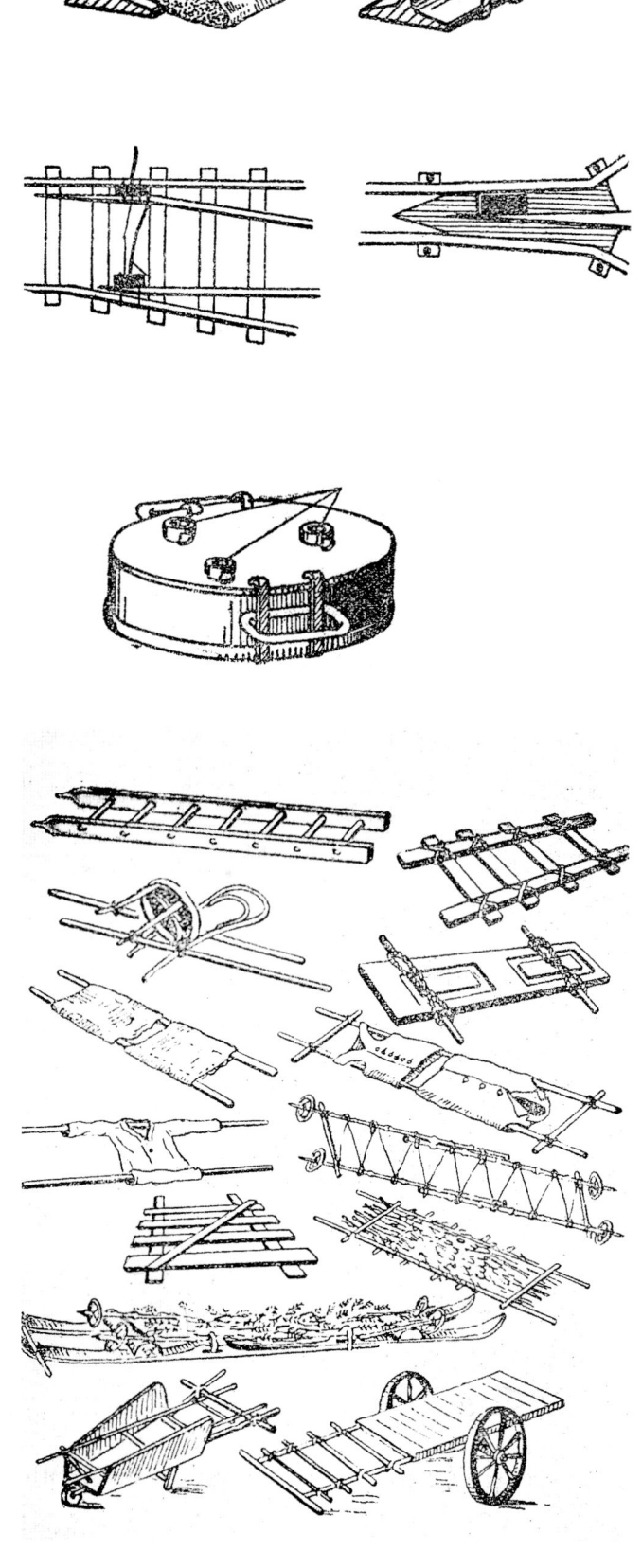

(Right) General arrangement drawing of a Soviet 82cm mortar, with a barrel about 48ins long. A number of different models were in service, including the BM-37 and BM-41; they were basically similar, although the later BM-43 model had two wheels attached to the baseplate for ease of movement. Even without them this class of weapon could be carried across country in three man-loads each weighing about 35-40lbs – although several other men were needed to carry a useful supply of its 7½lb high explosive bombs, which were rapidly expended in action due to a firing rate of up to 20 rounds per minute. By the second half of the war partisan units had more heavy weapons, even artillery pieces in some cases; but the mortar was probably the most useful, for its simplicity, ease of transport, and versality of use.

(Below) A Red Army mortar crew undergoing an inspection, 1944.

This is the heavy 120mm HM-38 mortar, of which at least 100 were meant to be issued to an artillery mortar brigade within each rifles division. It was so effective that the Wehrmacht used many captured examples designated GrW 378(r), and later actually manufactured an improved copy, the 12cm sGrW. Note the crewmen with Mosin carbines slung on their backs. The khaki field quality visored cap is worn not only by the officers (second left & far right), but also by the starshina sergeant-major (centre) and the mortar commander – probably a yefreitor *private first class* (left). The enlisted men wear ankle boots and the officers and starshina long boots. The inspecting officers and the sergeant-major wear full orders and medals. The senior lieutenant (second left) has the early officers' belt equipment with two shoulder braces.

The largest mortar used by the Red Army was the wheeled, towed M1943 of 160mm calibre; it fired 88lb bombs, uniquely loaded into an opening breech rather than down the muzzle.

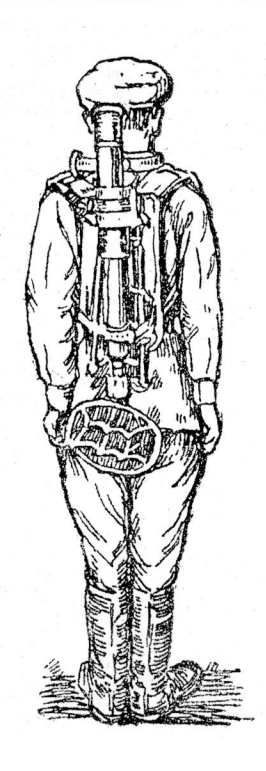

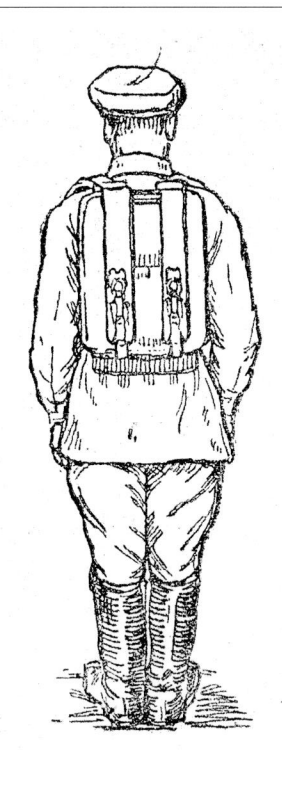

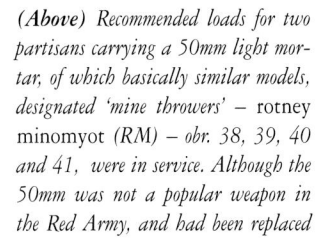

(Above) Recommended loads for two partisans carrying a 50mm light mortar, of which basically similar models, designated 'mine throwers' – rotney minomyot (RM) – obr. 38, 39, 40 and 41, were in service. Although the 50mm was not a popular weapon in the Red Army, and had been replaced in rifles units by 82mm mortars by the end of 1944, its light weight (not much more than 20lbs) and short length (about 22ins) made it handy for partisans, who needed to be highly mobile on foot across rough terrain.

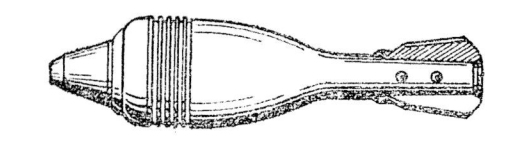

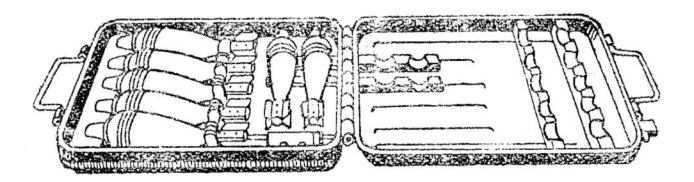

(Above) Mortar ammunition case for seven bombs. The 50mm round only weighed 1.9lbs, about a quarter the weight of the 82mm, and had a maximum range of only about 800 metres, against more than 3,000 metres for the 82mm.

(Below) A wrecked German 82mm mortar position; the tube, ammunition and cases for this class of weapon were almost identical in both armies. As the Red Army advanced many trenches were simply filled in as the graves for dead soldiers together with their wrecked weapons. In this trench corpses are probably buried just out of shot, since the photograph shows a characteristic scattering of white lime. Such hasty burials of men and ordnance caused deaths and injuries for decades after the war.

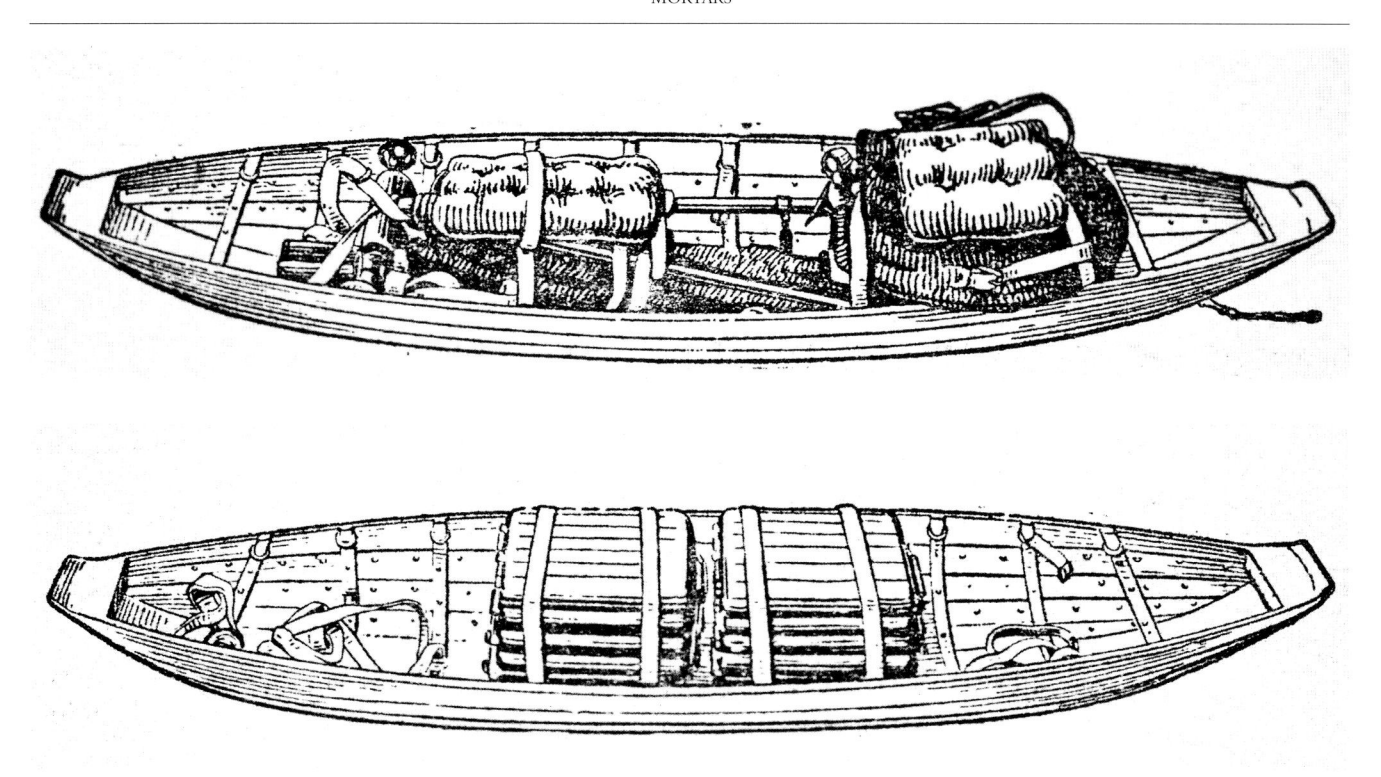

Partisans, often in small groups and very seldom with motor vehicles available, nevertheless had to transport mortars and large quantities of ammunition across country, including deep snow or swamps. The winter warfare manual showed examples of stowage for light boats or sleds (pulled by men or dogs) for this purpose, although such refinements would not have been widely available in the first years of the war.

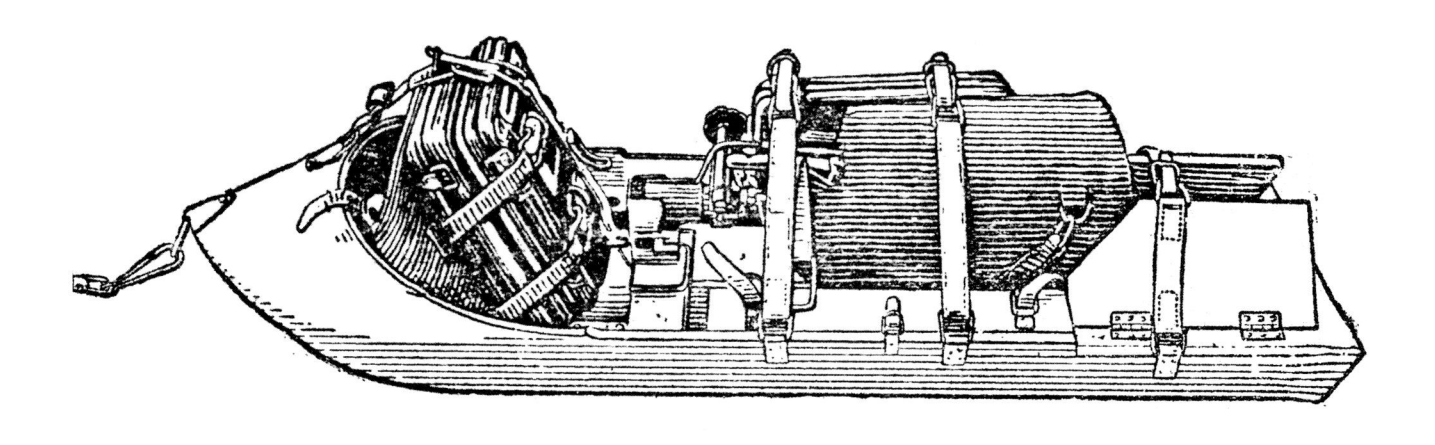

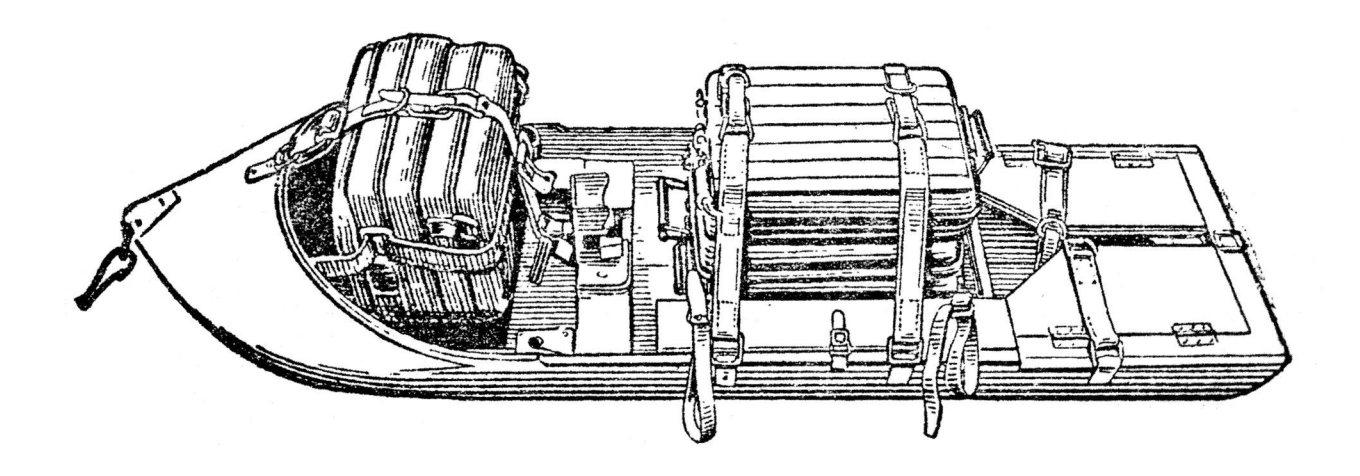

TACTICAL MANUALS

EARLY WAR TACTICAL MANUALS

(Above) The disastrous battle performance of the Red Army in summer 1941 was due partly to Stalin's savage pre-war purges of the officer corps, which left most units and formations commanded by men of limited experience and competence, and terrified of making any decision without higher authority; and partly simply to the lack of properly trained personnel in the ranks. Several manuals were created immediately, with the minor or major errors which such haste made inevitable. These covered subjects from general tactical principles, down to the handling of specific weapons and vehicles, and specific instruction in particular manoeuvres such as river crossings.

Soviet strategy was based on huge mass armies with basic military training, while air, airborne and naval operations played strictly subordinate roles. This was the inevitable doctrine of a vast land power with limited coastal harbours; but it was outdated, relying on massed infantry operations with low levels of tank and air support and little skilled specialist manpower. This failure to modernise cost the unnecessary death or capture of millions of soldiers in 1941–42.

On these pages we show extracts from the manual for winter and mountain warfare published in 1942. The drawings are self-explanatory; they show roping up, safe methods for traversing ledges and crossing glaciers, use of the iceaxe, and a snow shelter (with soldiers armed unconvincingly with a Tokarev semi-automatic rifle – a distant dream for most infantrymen at this date). The whole manual follows this very basic approach, assuming neither intelligence nor initiative: there is even a whole page of drawings demonstrating the approved methods of grasping handholds.

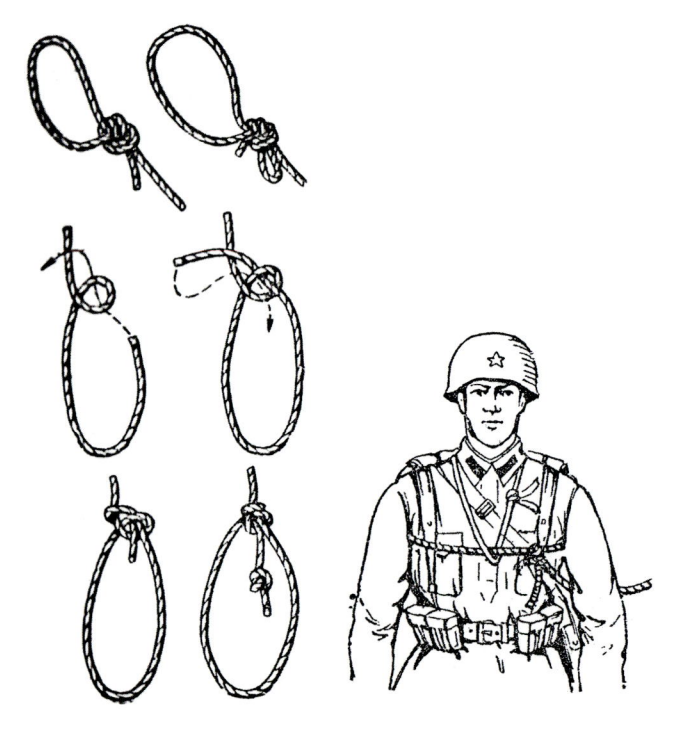

— 66 —

TACTICAL MANUALS

ARTILLERY CAPTAIN, TRANSCAUCASIAN MILITARY DISTRICT, SUMMER 1942

Wide-brimmed cotton tropical hats for wear in hot climates were introduced for all ranks of the Red Army in 1938 – much earlier than in most other armies. The territory of the Soviet Union covered environments with enormous ranges of heat and cold, humidity and aridity, altitude, terrain and vegetation. The Red Army made more extensive provision for extreme cold weather than for heat, since truly tropical conditions existed only in the far south and east, and changes to uniform were therefore limited. This so-called 'Panama' hat was often permitted for use with an opened gymnastiorka *collar, and sometimes with ankle boots. The gymnastiorka illustrated here is of a lightweight pale khaki material.*

This artillery captain, probably a battalion commander, is identified by the subdued metal branch insignia and rank bar on the khaki field collar patches ordered in April 1941; these were far from universal, and full-colour M1935 patches continued to be used very widely on field uniforms. He retains the officers' blue sharovary *breeches with red seam piping, and high boots. His weapon is the TT M1930 semi-automatic pistol, holstered on the officers' belt with its cut-out star buckle; the shoulder braces of this 'Sam Browne' design have been removed here. Note the light canvas field binocular case of wartime manufacture, with a leather lid and strapping; and the ubiquitous gasmask bag, used as a field haversack by all ranks.*

ARTILLERY CAPTAIN, CAUCASUS, SUMMER 1942

(Right) Detail of the field collar patches; note also the relatively coarse weave of the lightweight pale khaki material of the blouse. The SSh-40 steel helmet has its usual webbing chinstrap, and this one has random daubs of camouflage paint over the olive factory finish. This shlem was of simplified shape, making it easier and cheaper to manufacture than the M1936; the latter's applied 'comb' or crest at the top rear of the skull, which had no practical value, was discontinued, and so was the large open red star stencil on the front.

(Left) Rear view of the hat, gymnastiorka, breeches and equipment, with the helmet slung on the gasmask bag.

(Right) Examples of unobtrusive but interesting markings on uniform and equipment items. It is always poignant to find reminders of individual soldiers in collected items. In rare cases one may even find, inside helmet liners or behind ushanka ear flaps, farewell letters and testaments prepared in case of a soldier's death.

The Red Army button made by Rex of New Rochelle, NY, is an example of the humblest of the millions of Lend-Lease items supplied by the Allies during the war, ranging from cans of Spam to tanks and aircraft, and transported on Allied cargo ships in hazardous convoys to either the arctic ports of northern Russia, or to the Persian Gulf and the beginning of the southern overland route via Iran.

Wartime Red Army items are only sparsely stamped, but individual soldiers naturally marked their own kit in a variety of ways. One popular method was to write the name in bleech, as in this trigger-finger mitten once carried by a soldier named Nikolayev.

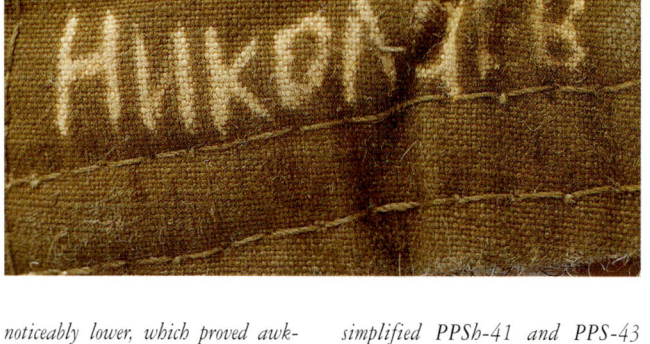

(Above) Scratched into the leather of this SMG magazine pouch are both the Red Army star, and the Islamic star-and-crescent – a reminder of the hundreds of thousands of soldiers from the ethnic groups of the Caucasian and Central Asian Soviet Republics. In proportion to more élite branches of service, ethnic minorities were over-represented in the ranks of the infantry. Their career prospects were limited by the inadequacy of their military training, political education and Russian language skills – and also by prejudice.

(Below) Page from a training manual showing the M1940 PPD and M1941 PPSh sub-machine guns. V.A.Degtyarev designed his first SMG in 1934; the PPD-34 was the same as the PPD-40 illustrated (top), but the wooden forestock was continuous. The drum magazine was thus mounted noticeably lower, which proved awkward in practice. Degtyarev corrected this in the PPD-40 and later SMGs, so that the magazine fitted directly under the receiver; even so, when firing such weapons from the prone position this arrangement is not ideal. The PPD was gradually replaced with the simplified PPSh-41 and PPS-43 models. G.S.Shpagin designed the barrel of the PPSh to be exactly half the length of the Mosin rifle barrel – while stocks lasted, PPSh production used cut-down barrels from original M1891 Mosins.

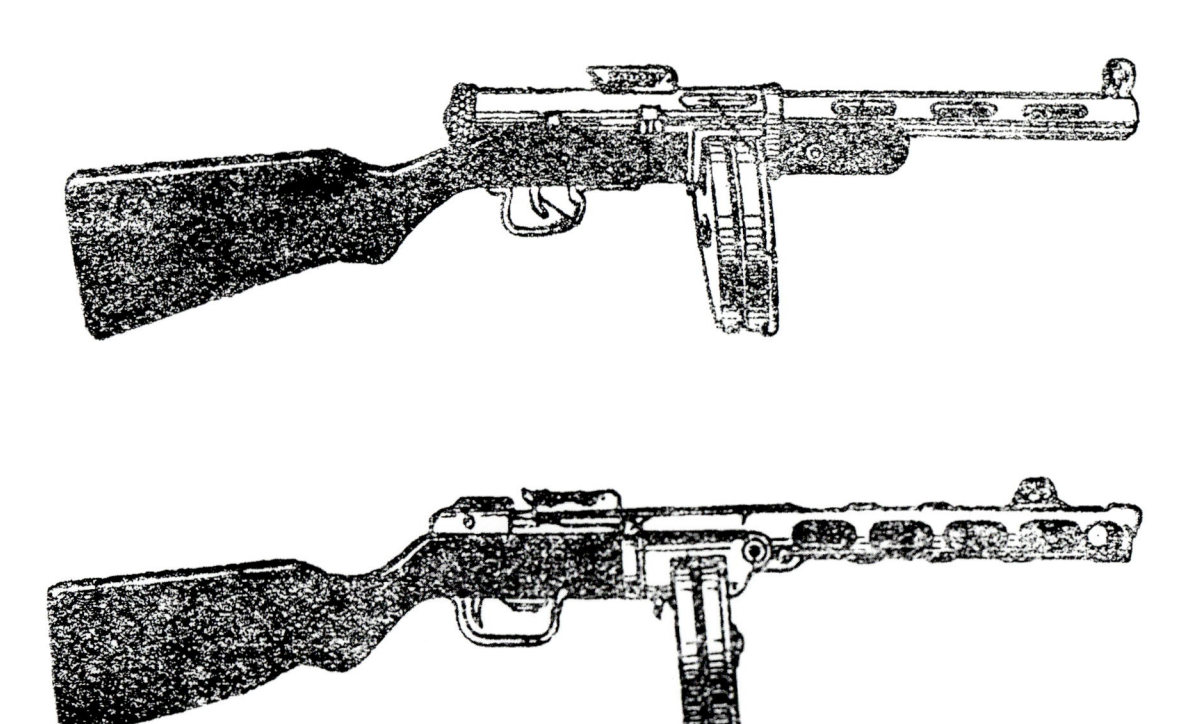

SUB-MACHINE GUNNER, 1942/43

This *krasnoarmeyets*, *preparing a hasty position in a building in Stalingrad during the final closing of the noose around the German 6th Army, wears the now-standard M1940 steel helmet, a padded jacket and khaki breeches. Note the usual muzzle-down position for carrying the PPSh-41 SMG slung, dictated by the 4lb weight of its 71-round drum magazine; this weapon reached the front in 1942. His field equipment is simple: a bag-like* veshmeshok *backpack, a canteen on his left hip in front of the gasmask satchel, a khaki canvas magazine pouch on the right, and – unusually – an entrenching tool.*

In soldiers' service books it is sometimes striking to read how few items of equipment had been issued to enlisted men and even officers. Sometimes soldiers were sent to the front with a full set of clothing and equipment – helmet, backpack, gasmask bag, entrenching tool, knife, etc.; but sometimes the only items listed are a belt and a padded jacket.

(**Below left**) *Handily placed immediately in front (left) of the trigger of the PPSh-41 is the selective fire lever, for changing between semi- and fully automatic fire.*

(**Below**) *A belt pouch for a PPSh drum magazine made in 1941, from an unusual grey shade of canvas. This colour was used for some items made for the arctic and mountain regions; white magazine pouches were also produced, though mostly for Mosin rifle clips.*

DT MACHINE GUN TEAM, STALINGRAD, EARLY 1943

(Above & opposite) The last days of the Stalingrad counter-offensive in February 1943 saw the first priority distributions to front line units of the shoulder boards of the January 1943 regulations (although the old collar patch rank system was still in use months later). Note the typical differences in appearance between these two soldiers. Some in the front lines made a point of displaying insignia and decorations on field uniforms and even on padded jackets, such as full-colour everyday shoulder boards, Guards badges and medals. This naturally made them more visible in combat; experienced fighters often remained as drably anonymous as they could, keeping insignia and decorations for wear when out of the line.

Pilotkas, ushankas and helmets were all worn in combat, and this was not always due to seasonal differences. Both ushankas and greatcoats are sometimes seen in summer photographs, and pilotkas in winter, because of constant shortages (and also because winter items were often used as blankets and pillows). Note, however, that by this date both soldiers have been issued with proper insulated mittens.

Their weapons are the PPSh-41 SMG, and the 7.62mm DT machine gun. The DT (see also pages 124–125) was originally mounted in tanks, but its good features, particularly for urban warfare – e.g. a small but capacious drum magazine and an adjustable shoulder stock – were soon recognized, and it was fitted with a bipod and modified sights for infantry use.

(Left, above) Detail of early button-and-loop fastening on a padded jacket; and, on the left breast, a scarlet wound stripe.

(Left) Wound stripes were introduced in the summer of 1942; they were to be worn above the right breast pocket, or in the equivalent position on garments without pockets. There were two versions: gold or yellow for serious wounds, and red for lighter injuries. Since issue stripes were often unobtainable in the front lines, from 1943 soldiers sometimes improvised with the rank stripes from sergeants' shoulder boards – red from field quality, and yellow from everyday/parade boards. Previously there had been no award specifically for wounds, although the Red Star Order and some others were often given in dual recognition of bravery and wounds.

DT MACHINE GUN TEAM, STALINGRAD, EARLY 1943

(*Above*) An example of the wartime Guards badge, of 1942 pattern; and (*above right*) two post-war pieces. Guard status was awarded – from September 1941 – to divisions that distinguished themselves in prolonged combat, and replaced a short-lived system of naming the division after the battle in which it had earned fame. Guard status brought extra pay to all ranks, priority for promotions and new equipment, and the right to be addressed as e.g. 'Comrade Guardsman'. The badge itself was introduced in March 1942. Wartime badges are easily recognized by the plain bottom edge to the banner, and the plain surface beneath its red enamelling. Post-1945 badges show a line of gold fringe along the bottom of the banner, and often a wavy machined pattern under the red enamel. Another clue may be found on the screw back; old examples are brass, engraved with uneven lettering.

(*Below*) Another distinction introduced from 1942 to improve morale was the series of high-quality enamelled 'Excellence' badges to reward individuals qualifying in various specialist military skills. Those shown here, below a wartime Guards badge, are (top, left to right:) Excellent Reconnaissance Soldier, Machine-gunner, Armoured Soldier, Artilleryman; (bottom:) Signaller, Air Defence Soldier, Medical Specialist.

RIFLES OFFICER, WINTER 1943

This junior officer wears a shuba sheepskin coat, with field shoulder boards attached. The animal-skin shuba, usually associated with officers and other privileged personnel, gave superior insulation to man-made fabrics; and the range of pale colours in which it came were also ideal for snowy conditions. His ushanka hat of high quality Persian lamb bears the usual red star cap badge. Note the officers' cut-out star belt buckle, officially an item of everyday/parade dress but one which was popular in the front line as a sign of officer status. The rest of an officer's field equipment was often very similar to that of his men, though map cases and binoculars were usually added. The sheepskin-lined gloves tucked under his belt were probably traded from a motorcyclist or tank crewman. His sidearm is the M1930 TT pistol, and he also carries the Sudayev PPS-43 sub-machine gun.

(Below) *A group mostly wearing the sheepskin* shuba, *1943. Note the fastening, by cord loops over big bone buttons, convenient for gloved fingers; the attached shoulder boards worn by four officers; and the black* kubanka *hat (rear right), of the type then worn by Cossacks, other cavalry, and also NKVD troops.*

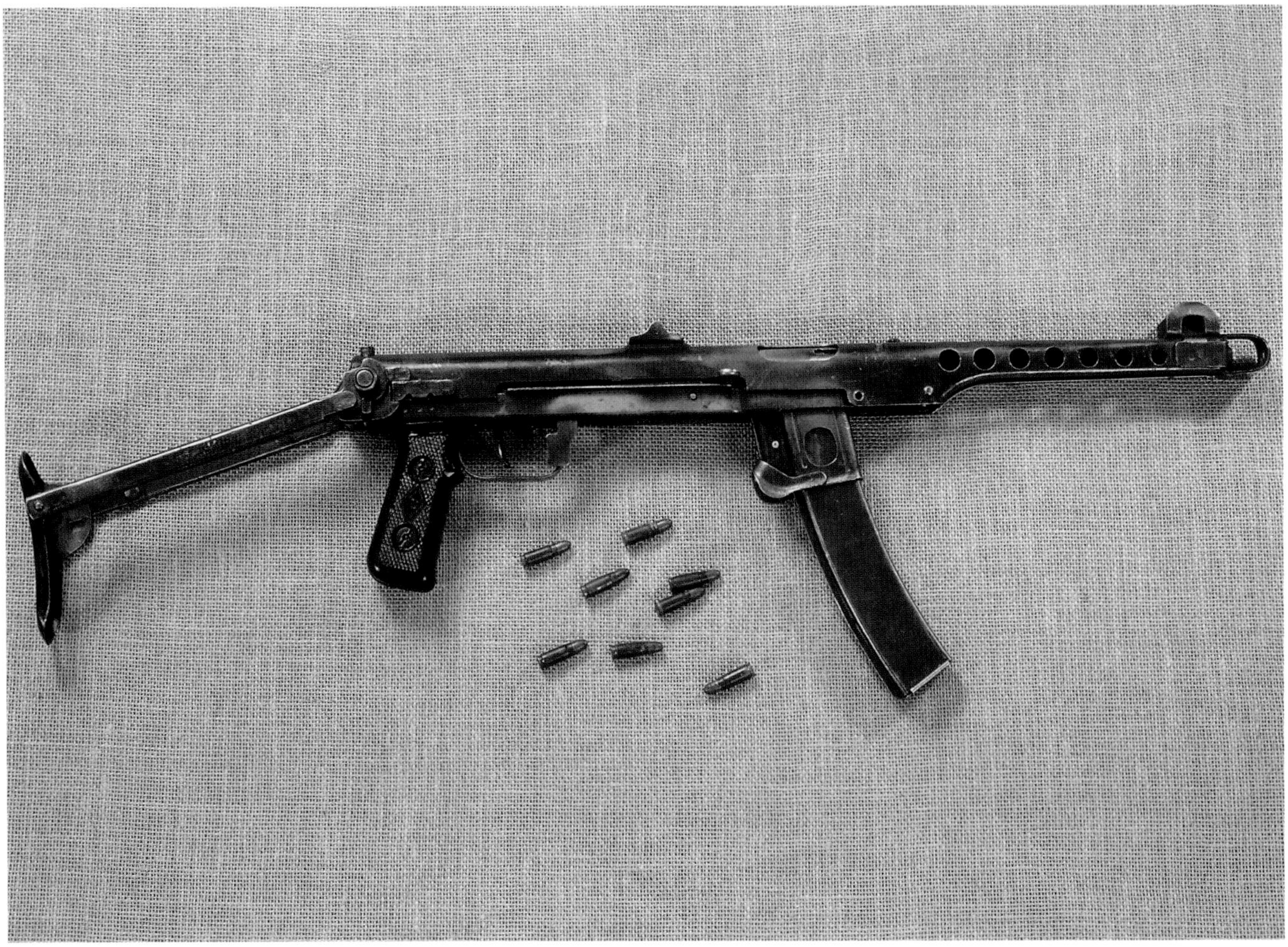

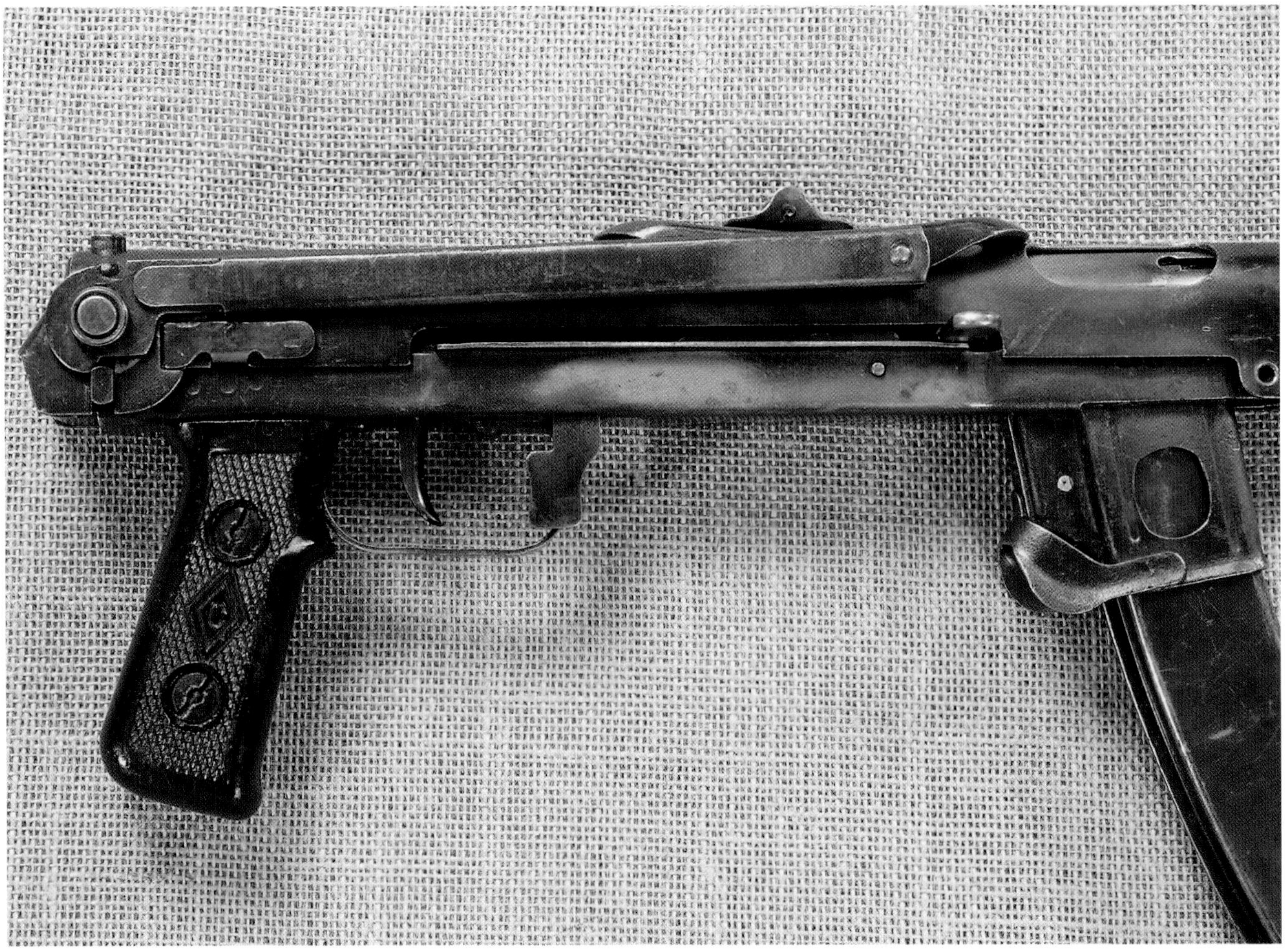

(Left) Cyrillic 'S' marking – Roman 'C' – for Sudayev, on the top surface of a PPS-43 dated 1944. The 'S' is also moulded in a diamond cartouche on the bakelite pistol grip.

(Below) A canvas magazine pouch for the box magazines. Several completely different versions were made (as in the case of many other such pouches). This piece has a simple, fragile bakelite button. Note the unusual sling, with a strangely shaped clasp probably designed for some other function. The white lining was also a war economy measure; black material was commonly used. The pouch was made to hold four magazines and a sectioned cleaning rod.

SUDAYEV SUB-MACHINE GUNS, PPS-42 AND PPS-43

The design engineer A.I.Sudayev was obliged to develop his sub-machine gun under the severe conditions of the siege of Leningrad, when all materials, energy supplies, technical facilities, skilled manpower (and the food to keep them alive) were in terribly short supply. The only advantage of the location was that experimental prototypes could be tested against the enemy only a few minutes' walk from the factory. The simplicity of the weapon was in accordance with both the need for easy and rapid manufacture, and the shortage of materials; during the planning of the production process, the wasted metal which would be cut away was reduced from 70 per cent to less than 50 per cent. There were several small modifications between the M1942 and the M1943: the earlier had wooden grips, soon replaced by rubber or bakelite in the PPS-43, and the M1942 had a longer skeleton stock. Both had the distinctive combined muzzle brake/compensator of curved metal sheet.

The simplicity, light construction, folding skeleton stock, and new curved 35-round box magazine all made the PPS a popular and handy weapon for 'tank-rider' infantry, reconnaissance units, and in urban combat. The box magazine and skeleton stock reduced the loaded weight to just under 8lbs, in contrast to the 12lbs of the PPSh-41.

All Soviet sub-machine guns of World War II used 7.62mm × 25mm pistol ammunition; and the PPS-43 barrel, at under 10ins even shorter than that of the PPSh-41, also contributed to the short effective range of about 50 metres. However, the generous scale of issue of such weapons to assault troops was intended to encourage aggressive advances to within short range of the enemy; unlike its predecessor, Sudayev's sub-machine gun had no fire selection lever and only fired fully automatic, though its reduced rate of fire – 600rpm, against up to 900rpm for the PPSh-41 – gave better control.

(Opposite) The PPS-43 with stock extended, and folded – the locking catch is the large round button at the rear of the receiver. A large safety catch is located at the front of the trigger guard.

COSSACK MAJOR, SPRING 1943

The old-style uniform of the 1935 and 1940 regulations is still being worn, but probably not for much longer; the major's unit is clearly resting after being pulled out of the line, and he will shortly put up his new shoulder boards. His visored cap is in the traditional dark blue with red distinctions, as used throughout the cavalry. The outdated gymnastiorka has large patch breast pockets, and – not unusually in combat units – the collar patches have been removed. Note the Guards badge in its usual position, fastened through the buttonhole of the right pocket flap. His rank is indicated only by the forearm chevrons in gold on red.

Blue sharovary breeches were to be seen in use by some cavalrymen until the end of the war, although long replaced by khaki in the other branches. Sometimes, though not in this reconstruction, cavalry sharovary had broad red seam stripes.

(Above) 1942-dated snapshot of a senior lieutenant of rifles troops, wearing essentially the same uniform as the reconstructed major opposite, apart from the khaki cap with the rifles' raspberry-red band and piping. Note the rank badges of the July 1940 regulations: a red chevron-cut backing on both forearms of the gymnastiorka bears the three narrow gold chevrons of senior lieutenant; and his gold-edged, raspberry-red collar patches bear the branch badge of crossed rifles set on a white target, behind the three red-enamelled squares of his rank.

(Above right) Detail of the M1932 cavalry commander's belt equipment, with whistle pouch on the left shoulder brace and the whistle strap passing back over the shoulder.

(Right) The lash or quirt is a personal item, which in Cossack use dated from centuries back in Imperial times.

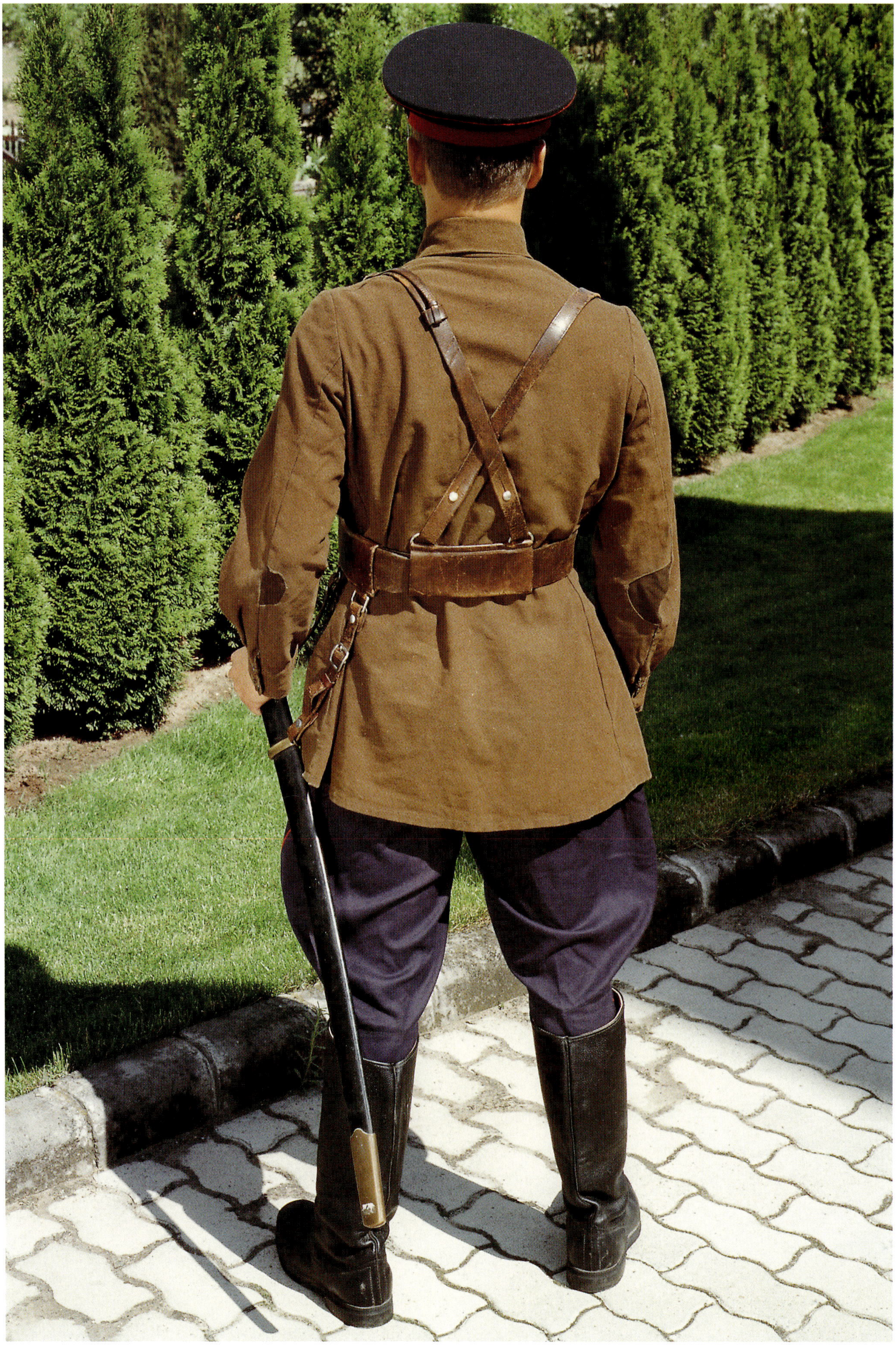

COSSACK MAJOR, SPRING 1943

(Above) Rear detail of the belt kit, showing the method of attaching the shoulder braces, and the suspension for the scabbard of the shashka sabre. Only the rear strap from the scabbard's belt loop is a suspension sling, the front one being simply a steadying strap to the hilt.

(Above right) Here the major wears an early model large wristwatch for commanders. Note also detail of rank chevrons, and shashka hilt.

(Opposite) General rear view (note repairs to both elbows of this gymnastiorka). The whistle strap passes over the left shoulder and attaches to the rear of the brace.

(Right) As an alternative, we substitute here a field compass on a wrist strap. On the face of the dial at bottom left can just be made out 'RKKA', for Workers' and Peasants' Red Army.

81

THE COSSACKS

Who, exactly, were the Cossacks? They were not ethnic minorities, but the descendants of a loosely defined class of people who first appeared in the chronicles of the early 16th century.

At that date the Russian royal state consisted of a limited area around Moscow itself – Muscovy. Within its borders most common people lived in powerless serfdom, ruled by feudal nobles and later by the centralized government of the Tsars. Over many years large numbers of the more adventurous rural peasants emigrated east and south, to found their own independent communities in the wilderness. Here, around the rivers of the interior – the Dniepr, the Don, the Kuban, and ultimately the Terek – they evolved a rough form of social equality, and their communities slowly coalesced into major regional 'hosts'. The Cossacks prided themselves on their independence and vigour, while the Russian authorities regarded them as pestilential outlaws, bandits and raiders.

As Muscovy gradually expanded, and after many wars, the Tsarist governments and the Cossack hosts reached an accommodation. The Cossack horsemen played a major part in exploring beyond the Urals; meanwhile they farmed the borderlands, and in time of trouble their skills as irregular cavalry proved invaluable – not only against external enemies, but also against the Tsars' other rebellious subjects. They enjoyed freedoms and privileges unknown to the common Russian peasantry, and their colourful folk culture celebrated their daring and masculinity in dancing and song. In the 19th century, from the defeat of Napoleon to the wars of expansion into Central Asia, their fame spread world-wide.

As the Tsar's 'most loyal hounds', the Cossacks were sent to draw sabres against the liberal revolutionaries of 1905–07, and against the far more dangerous Bolsheviks in 1917 and during the devastating Civil War that followed; very few of them went over to the 'Reds'. After the defeat of the loyalists many of them emigrated, and their communities were ruthlessly persecuted or deported far from their lands: not only had they fought for the 'Whites', but they were natural enemies of the Communist state – agriculturally successful *kulaks* or 'rich peasants', proud of their old, independent ways.

When the German forces slashed deep into the USSR in 1941–42, large numbers of Cossacks – among hundreds of thousands of other Soviet subjects – were recruited by the invaders to fight against their former oppressors. It may therefore seem strange that significant cavalry formations were also raised for the Red Army; but the reforms of late 1942 and 1943 came just in time. The Soviet state recognized that the patriotic power of folk traditions was a better motivating force than cold and confusing ideology, and harnessed the Cossacks' Tsarist history in the service of Mother Russia.

(Opposite top) Cossack and cavalry visored cap, in the traditional dark blue and red. Note the double chin-strap, one functional and one decorative, as used when on horseback (and also by the Fleet, for the same practical reason).

(Opposite bottom) Shashka sabres, dated 1942 (top) and 1923. The troopers carried rifles, and the enlisted ranks' scabbard was always fitted with a holder for the Mosin bayonet. Note that the pre-war wooden scabbard is covered with fine black leather and has a brass chape and throat, while the wartime economy model is covered with canvas and has cheap iron fittings. The early hilt is chiseled with a star, hammer-and-sickle, trophies, and the legend 'CCCP'; the 1942 piece is roughly stamped with a single star. The wartime sabre was made in besieged Leningrad at the Kirov Factory (named after the city's popular Party Secretary, whom the mistrustful Stalin had had assassinated. The Kirov factory had originally been the Putilov works, a hotbed of political activity in the 1917 revolution.)

Since the Militia did not use truncheons, former cavalry shashkas were still issued to police units until the late 1950s.

(Above) A shashka modified for a left-handed cavalryman by moving the bayonet holder to the other side of the scabbard. Note the (also irregular) sword knot, common in World War 1 but hardly seen under the Communists. After the Cossacks' Mosin rifles were replaced with PPSh-41 SMGs the scabbard lost its bayonet fittings.

(Below) Markings on Imperial (left & centre) and Soviet-made (right) shashkas. The Cossacks used Imperial stocks while they lasted; later Soviet production added Soviet symbols to weapons of the same size and style. The simple star stamp on the hilt (below right) is from the 1942 Leningrad economy version.

To produce such non-essential items as traditional sabres, at a time of starvation and shortages of modern firearms, was a symbolic act of defiance to support fighting morale at a time of agony. In the old capital of the Tsars, icons of the Virgin Mary were carried through the trenches to encourage the defenders of the Motherland in the old way; and in 1943 all the main streets got their pre-Soviet names back.

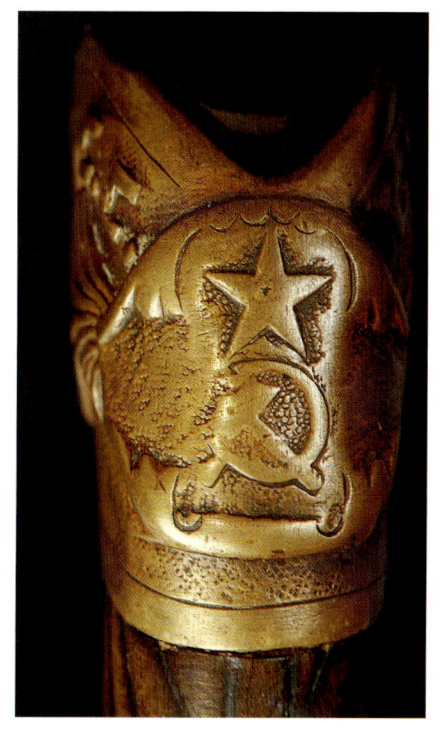

FROM COLLAR PATCHES TO SHOULDER BOARDS

(Right) Two majors pose for a studio portrait in 1942, still clearly displaying the full colour collar patches of the December 1935 regulations on the fall-collar gymnastiorka.

The officer on the left wears the old two-brace belt arrangement, and his dark blue *sharovary* can just be seen. His black collar patches, edged with gold, bear the crossed cannons of the artillery and the two bars of his rank; the Order of the Red Star, for personal bravery or a serious wound, is pinned to his left breast.

The major on the right, displaying the Order of the Red Banner, wears no branch emblem on the collar patches.

(Below) To judge from the immaculate condition of their greatcoats, this senior lieutenant and lieutenant photographed in March 1943 have just received them, complete with the new rank insignia ordered under Prikaz 25 that January. The actual process of change was gradual, over several months. The lieutenant (right) still wears the old fall-collar gymnastiorka under his coat, but without the old collar patches; his oversized coat is wrongly fastened right-over-left. The new greatcoat collar patches were in branch-of-service colours and pipings (officially, gold for officers), but bore a single button rather than rank and branch insignia. The lieutenant apparently wears the scarlet-piped black patches of tank or artillery enlisted ranks, but both officers have khaki field shoulder boards edged raspberry-red; and the right-hand man has attached to his the old infantry rifles-and-target emblem formerly worn on his collar patches and now officially abolished. (Incidentally, note these fine examples of period haircuts.)

(**Right**) A selection of shoulder boards, 1943–45.

As already remarked, those termed 'everyday' quality were for walking-out and parade uniforms. For officers these boards were faced in either gold or silver lace (combat or non-combat), showing edging in various branch colours; these sometimes, but not usually, differed in colour from the single or double lengthways stripes which, in conjunction with the number of stars, identified exact ranks. Everyday shoulder boards for enlisted ranks were in branch colours, with branch piping at the edges, and sometimes with unit cyphers; NCO ranks were identified by added cloth transverse stripes for corporals, sergeants and senior sergeants, and by a T-shaped arrangement for sergeant-majors. Field quality shoulder boards had a khaki ground for all ranks. The examples in this photograph are all everyday quality unless otherwise noted.

(Top row:) colonel, artillery; major, engineers; supply major, NKVD; major, medical service.
(Centre:) senior lieutenant, artillery; lieutenant, signals (black edging was also used by chemical defence and some engineers); field quality – junior lieutenant, rifles; senior lieutenant, supply corps (while the NKVD supply officer is in a combat unit, and so has gold lace, this officer is in a non-combat supply unit, so has silver).
(Bottom:) senior sergeant, NKVD; field quality – sergeant, Air Force; private, rifles (raspberry-red, black piping, yellow unit cypher); Militiaman (dark blue, light blue piping, gold unit cypher).

(**Below**)
(Top row, left to right:) colonel of a non-combat branch; major, supply corps, combat formation; field quality – major, artillery; field quality – major, medical service; major, medical, for women's white parade tunic; senior lieutenant, administration; senior lieutenant, rifles; senior lieutenant, artillery; lieutenant, chemical defence.
(Bottom row:) Field quality – sergeant-major, Air Force; senior sergeant, rifles; field quality – private, artillery (scarlet piping, rather than rifles raspberry-red).

A fine example of an 'everyday' quality officer's shoulder board for parade and walking-out uniform: major of cavalry, with blue edging and two rank stripes, rank star and cavalry branch emblem.

IDENTIFYING SHOULDER BOARDS

After several years of careful study, a collector or researcher may believe that he or she has completely mastered the rank and branch systems of the Soviet armed forces, and can identify with confidence any piece, estimating its period of issue and wear – particularly the collar patches of the 1935 and 1940 regulations, and the shoulder boards introduced under the January 1943 reforms. However, there is always scope for confusion when one encounters a previously unseen example with minor variations. This brief discussion does not pretend to explain, for instance, the innumerable variations of cyphers which may be found on shoulder boards, which would take a lifetime to collect and a book of this size to document; it is devoted simply to the major headings for identification.

Wide or narrow?

One of the most puzzling questions is simply, why are some shoulder boards that apparently identify the same rank and branch wide, and some – for instance, of the medical and veterinary services – narrow?

Narrow shoulder boards – 4cm–4.5cm wide – indicated that the officer had completed higher education (normally at university level) in a non-military field of study – e.g. medicine, economics, law, etc. – but had not passed through military academy. In these branches, the wearers of conventional 6cm-wide shoulder boards had both military and civil professional qualifications. Such officers had either completed separately both military academy and higher studies in one of the above-mentioned disciplines; or had graduated from a specialised military academy in that discipline, qualifying to be both, for instance, a military surgeon and a commander in the military medical service.

Branch of service colours

As a general rule, the branches of service were shown on everyday-quality shoulder boards by the colour combination: the base colour, and the edging or piping (and for officers, the lengthways rank stripes underlying the applied rank stars). The officers' metallic lace, of gold for combat branches/formations and silver for non-combat, was woven in continuous rolls incorporating the coloured rank stripes, usually cut to a length of between 14cm and 16cm, and sewn down on the coloured underlays, leaving these visible as edging. Enlisted ranks had shoulder boards entirely of the branch colour, piped usually in contrasting colours. The basic range of branch colours was as follows (O = officers' edging and rank stripes if the same; OE = officers' edging if different from rank stripes; ER = enlisted ranks' base colour/piping:)
Rifles (infantry) O raspberry-red; *ER* raspberry-red/black
Artillery O scarlet; *ER* black/scarlet
Armoured troops O scarlet; *ER* black/scarlet
Cavalry O blue; *ER* blue/black
Engineers O scarlet, *OE* black; *ER* black/black
Signals O raspberry-red, *OE* black; *ER* black/black
Air Force O light blue; *ER* light blue/black
Medical O scarlet; *ER* dark green/scarlet

On khaki field quality shoulder boards the enlisted ranks' edge piping was of the main branch colour, e.g. raspberry-red for rifles, scarlet for artillery and tank troops, blue for cavalry, light blue for Air Force, and so on. It is therefore not always possible to distinguish between all branches in all cases.

Emblems and cyphers

Additionally, the branch was identified by emblems, the miniature badges symbolic of that branch's duties, often featuring weapons or tools – e.g. a tank, crossed cannon barrels, crossed rifles, crossed swords on a horseshoe, crossed axes for engineers, a serpent-and-goblet for the medical branch, etc. The emblems were worn on shoulder boards, by officers close to the collar just outside the button, and by enlisted ranks further out towards the end.

While the regulations mentioned cyphers in the form of unit numbers or identifying letters to be displayed on the shoulder boards of enlisted ranks, in practice these were rarely seen. In theory the shoulder boards bore, from the button outwards, any appropriate rank stripes, the branch emblem, and numbers or letters. Some examples of the cyphers displayed on enlisted ranks' everyday full colour shoulder boards are as follows:
Regiments of rifles, artillery, cavalry, engineers, etc. The number of the regiment only.
Guard regiments Cyrillic 'G' after number.
Guard anti-tank artillery regiments Cyrillic 'GP' after number.
Guard tank brigades Cyrillic 'GB' after number.
Mortar regiments Cyrillic 'M' after number.
Motorcyclists Tank troops' shoulder boards, Cyrillic 'M' after number.
Air Force bomber regiments Cyrillic 'B' after number.
Air Force Guard fighter regiments Cyrillic 'GI' after number.

Special schools

The Suvorov Schools were set up from autumn 1943 for orphans of the Great Patriotic War, offering basic care and education, and also patriotic indoctrination. Their red shoulder boards bore the first two Cyrillic characters of the name of the town where the school was located, and outside this the Cyrillic letters 'SVU'.

The Special Military Secondary Schools were created from 1938, but in autumn 1943 they received new uniforms and shoulder boards. These schools were established especially for non-Russian pupils from the other Soviet Republics, in order both to improve their career opportunities and to integrate them into the Red Army as a loyal élite for the future. The curriculum placed heavy emphasis on the Russian language and mathematics. The students' shoulder boards were in branch colours with broad yellow or silver lace edging, like those of the *kursants* at military academies but in a narrower version; they bore the number of the school and the Cyrillic 'Ssh' abbreviation.

Other school cyphers were 'PU' for Military Polytechnics, and 'S' for the Stalin Air Force Technical School.

The NKVD

The *Narodny Kommissariat Vnutrennikh Del* or People's Commissariat for Internal Affairs was a complex organisation responsible for many departments apart from the basic State Security service. The NKVD did form strong military units and formations – about 15 rifle divisions in 1941, rising to 53 divisions and 28 separate brigades by 1945; and these were sometimes committed to the front lines (for instance, in the liberation of the Crimea in 1944). However, they were most often seen in the second line, forcibly preventing any wavering by Red Army units; and their usual role was in repressive security operations as part of the Internal Troops – hunting down anti-Soviet partisans, and carrying out mass deportations of suspect ethnic minorities. The NKVD Frontier Guards (branch colour green, with raspberry-red piping) were an important and separate military force, which boasted not only infantry but also some artillery and armour, and were heavily involved in the first defensive campaigns in particular. A few examples of the cyphers authorised for the everyday shoulder boards of enlisted ranks are as follows:

Frontier Guard units Unit number only.
Frontier Guard detached HQs Cyrillic letters 'OK' after number.
Internal Forces (special units):
Railway troops Cyrillic letter 'Zh' after number.
Convoy escorts Cyrillic letter 'K' after number.
Militia Cyrillic letter 'O' after number. Sometimes an abbreviation of the police station or the function were also shown, so there were a huge number of variations.
Prison guards Cyrillic letters 'MZ', but not the prison number.
GULAG labour camp guards Cyrillic letters 'OL', but again, no identification of a specific camp (which officially may not have existed).
Militarised fire brigade Cyrillic letters 'VPO' after unit number.

Naval flotilla cyphers

The named Fleets also displayed abbreviated cyphers, both on the full length Army-style shoulder boards and on the small tabs worn on the naval jumpers. To confuse the collector further, some rivers and lakes had their own flotillas identified by separate abbreviations. Some of the lesser-known examples are as follows, all in the usual Cyrillic characters:

Amur Flotilla 'AF'; *Caspian Sea Flotilla* 'KF'; *River Volga Flotilla* 'VF' (this played an important role during the battle for Stalingrad); *Lake Onega Flotilla* 'OF' (on the Finnish front); *Naval Engineering School* 'IT'; *Shore Defence Artillery School* 'BT'.

(Above) These broad lace edgings identify students at officers' academies. The base and piping colours reflect branches of service – here, rifles, supply corps, armour technical, and administration.

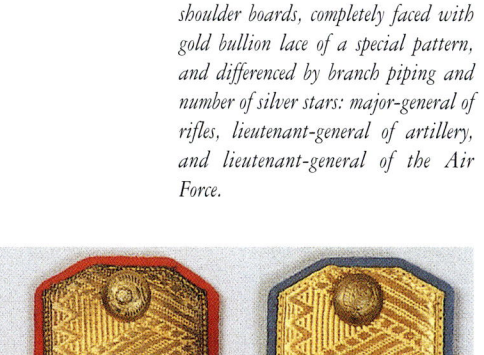

(Below) General officers' everyday shoulder boards, completely faced with gold bullion lace of a special pattern, and differenced by branch piping and number of silver stars: major-general of rifles, lieutenant-general of artillery, and lieutenant-general of the Air Force.

JOINT SOVIET-HUNGARIAN PATROL, BUDAPEST, WINTER, 1944/45

JOINT SOVIET-HUNGARIAN PATROL, BUDAPEST, WINTER, 1944/45

The destruction of the German 6th Army at Stalingrad in the first weeks of 1943 was the first turning-point of the war on the Eastern Front. The second came in July 1943, with the failure of the last great Wehrmacht offensive around Kursk; and the third in summer 1944, when a series of massive Soviet offensives smashed Germany's Army Group Centre and took the Red Army far to the west. Now they were fighting on foreign soil, in countries formerly occupied by or allied with the Nazis, and foreign troops were enlisted to fight on the Soviet side. In Hungary, now a battleground, a pro-Soviet provisional government formed at Debrecen called on Hungarian troops to support the Red Army; although this had little significant result, some Hungarians did respond.

(**Opposite**) Here a Red Army junior lieutenant, escorted by one of his soldiers, is guided through the rail yards by a Hungarian volunteer. The Hungarians used mixed clothing and equipment – civilian, Honved (Hungarian Royal Army), German and Soviet. This man wears the Hungarian bocskai cap with the national cockade and royal crown buttons removed. He has been issued the usual Soviet padded jacket and a Mosin rifle, and an identifying armband; an alternative was red or white cloth bands around the Hungarian M1935 helmet or other field headgear. The Soviet soldier, armed with a PPSh-41, has the M1940 helmet, and displays full colour rifles shoulder boards, a Guards badge and a wound stripe. His commander is distinguished by an officer's red-piped pilotka, and wears a plashch-palatka tent section over his uniform.

(**Below**) The M1938 waterproofed tent section/rain cape, of waxed cotton duck with a hood and arm slits, was officially termed the paladka-plashch-nakidka. It was widely used as part of the field uniform by all ranks in all weather conditions, as protection against rain, wind and cold and as a groundsheet. It also had some camouflage effect in blurring the soldier's silhouette, although produced only in various olive-khaki shades (in contrast to the equivalents produced by the Germans, Italians and Hungarians, who had already recognized the advantages of camouflage-patterned versions). Several sections – typically six – could be fastened together to make a bivouac tent. It was also used in a roll or bundle to carry ammunition, rations, and plunder (in some Warsaw Pact countries it was later called the 'pig-stealer'). In wartime photographs and film footage it is rare to see wounded being carried on wood- or metal-framed stretchers (litters); the tent section was almost universally used for carrying casualties out of the front line to the first aid posts or to vehicles.

A rubberised sleeveless raincoat with detachable hood was first used from 1954 – and then only by officers – and was officially mentioned only in the 1959 uniform regulations, much later than in other modern armies.

JOINT SOVIET-HUNGARIAN PATROL, BUDAPEST, WINTER, 1944/45

(Left & below) This rare armband is one version of those issued to the Hungarian 'People's Guard', bearing the Cyrillic title NARODNA STRAZHA; the individual number '394' shows that they were issued sparingly and against a nominal roll. Such armbands – also found with Hungarian script – were given to local people who welcomed the Red Army's arrival and actively supported them. Responsible for public order, and liaison between the Red Army and the local population, they were allowed to carry weapons and to patrol the streets after the evening curfew.

The Red Army made little use of armbands during the wartime years, although several different types were introduced in the post-war period. During the Great Patriotic War they were limited to Red Cross brassards for medics, and a simple letter 'P' (the Cyrillic 'R') for traffic control 'regulators'; even these were often hand-made. More similar to the illustrated armband were those identifying 'Russian Militia', sometimes with added sewn-on rank stripes.

(Left) Hungarian Partisan Medal. Although members of local resistance groups, trade unions, and left wing political organisations who had suffered persecution under the pro-Nazi régime came forward to assist the liberators, there had in fact been very few Hungarian partisans actively fighting against German and government troops before the Red Army's arrival. The Austro-Hungarian Empire had only collapsed some 20 years beforehand; in both World Wars a large proportion of Hungary's young men had fought on the German side on the Russian fronts; and in many areas men from so-called 'ethnic German' populations – a loosely applied definition – were still being conscripted by the Germans in 1944. However, as the socialist regime stabilized in the late 1940s and 1950s a number of people recognized the advantages of holding a medal confirming partisan status; just as in the USSR, medal-holders enjoyed privileges in accommodation, education, social and health services, official employment, and access to consumer goods. Increasing numbers of people claimed to have been partisans, often in large groups who gave each other mutual verification. Consequently the prestige of the medal was devalued, and with it the true heroism of the few who had a genuine claim to the status of wartime resisters.

There was a joke circulating in the 1980s about an old man claiming to have given food to the partisans and to have cared for and hidden their wounded. When the vetting committee asked him what the partisans had said to him, he replied, 'Oh, they said danke schön!'

PROPAGANDA

(Left) Propaganda postcard showing the meeting of Czechoslovakian and Soviet soldiers at the frontier. The Red Army men are presented as dominant in this group, which centres on a Russian sergeant at left foreground. The Czech soldiers do the work, digging a hole for the frontier sign as a symbol of sovereignty.

(Below) Czechoslovakian 50 crown banknote commemorating the meeting of Red Army troops and Slovakian partisans in the High Tatra mountains at the time of the Slovakian uprising against German, Hungarian and puppet Slovakian government troops in 1944. Its design is typical of its period, the early 1960s. The idealised Soviet sergeant and Slovakian partisan look like operetta stars, and despite the PPS-43 sub-machine gun and ushanka *the details are equally unconvincing. The star belt buckle was not used by enlisted ranks until 1951; and in 1944 pleated patch pockets on an enlisted man's* gymnastiorka *were exclusive to the NKVD. Again, the dominance of the smart, well-equipped Soviet soldier is stressed.*

— 91 —

(Above) The crew of a M1942 76.2mm ZiS-3 dual purpose gun reading some of the latest 'front newspapers'. Note the captured P08 Luger Parabellum pistol holstered on the right hip of the left-hand soldier – this was a popular battlefield trophy.

(Right) One aspect of the political directorate's 'agitation and propaganda' work was supplying motivational reading matter for the troops. It was common to see in the front line such publications as Pravda ('The Truth', newspaper of the Communist Party), Komsomolskaya Pravda (the journal of the Communist youth organisation), Voroshilovets (the Red Army newspaper, named after Marshal Voroshilov), Izvestiya (journal of the People's Deputies), and Za Nashu Pobeda ('For Our Victory', a Red Army daily newssheet). Usually these featured a prominent picture of Stalin, with one of his speeches or orders of the day, together with reports of some victorious operation.

GENERAL OFFICERS, 1944 (see overleaf)

(Page 93, & left) Major-generals, 1944. General officers had various official orders of dress, and photographs also show many deviations from the regulation uniforms. Typical personally acquired items included very high quality winter coats, boots, gloves and belts, as well as specially tailored tunics and breeches. These impressive variations from the norm had the obvious effect of raising prestige; but there was also an opposite tendency – in the field some generals and other senior officers reduced the marks of their status to the minimum. The generals' breeches with double (usually red) stripes, most commonly in dark blue sharovary style, were hardly seen in the combat zones. Coats without shoulder boards, and visored caps without the generals' gold chin cords or special cap badge, were not unusual. Medals and orders were also laid aside.

This major-general (above left, and page 93) has the simple single-breasted *kitel* tunic, with generals' red piping on the standing collar and the cuffs only. The five large gilt buttons bear the coat of arms of the USSR. He wears plain khaki winter field breeches without generals' stripes or even officers' piping. Although he wears everyday shoulder boards he does not display his medals and orders; in these circumstances an exception might be made for the supreme decoration, the gold star of a Hero of the Soviet Union. His boots are of officers' quality in fine soft leather.

(Above) A range of items which might be seen hanging in a command bunker in a cellar, 1944/45. The PPSh-41 hangs muzzle-down, to avoid accidents. The soldier's *shinel* greatcoat with an infantryman's field shoulder boards (left) may be used as a blanket, or for a senior officer's quick visit to the trenches. Note the khaki cap of field quality, with a plastic visor. The grey blanket with a black stripe (right) – like several other items favoured by any Soviet soldier who could lay hands on them – is probably a captured Romanian piece; note that the Red Army issued its troops with no blankets, expecting them to make do with the greatcoat and tent section/rain cape. (The Hungarian Army blanket was similar, with a lighter base colour and national red-white-green stripes.) Note the various map cases, and 6×30 or 8×30 field binoculars.

(Below left, & opposite top) Note the winter coat. This simple *bekesha* style field coat was introduced for command personnel only in 1931, especially in the Far East and Siberian Military Districts. At that date it was used without collar rank insignia. From 1943 shoulder boards were authorised but, as here, not always worn – note the loops for their attachment.

GENERAL OFFICERS, 1944

(Left) The buttons on the cuffs and the back are cloth-covered – a feature unique to this coat and the field quality visored cap. The coat was fastened with hooks-and-eyes, like the soldiers' *shinel* greatcoat. If this general fastens his coat the only external sign of his status will be the broad collar made of the same high quality grey lambskin as the *papaha* winter hat.

Sometimes in the trenches a brave and highly decorated senior NCO wearing a visored cap (e.g. see page 113) might look more like a general than did his more careful commander – and this might make the difference between life and death. However, the plain outfits chosen by some generals were not only to reduce their visibility to snipers; prestige was based upon their identification with the common *krasnoarmeyets*, and a personal reputation for bravery in sharing the dangers and hardships of the front lines.

(Below left) General officers' M1940 visored cap – one of the first steps in the differentiation between Red Army generals and marshals and less senior officers. It was the only kind of wartime cap with gold chin cords. This, and the generals' special two-piece cap badge, were introduced in 1940 in two versions: gold for combat branches, and silver for non-combatants – e.g. the medical and veterinary services, some non-field engineers and technical departments, the supply corps, administrative service, etc. The side buttons (also in either gold or silver) bore the coat of arms of the USSR. The basic colours and piping followed the branch of service; in wartime this black velvet band and scarlet piping were mostly worn by tank generals.

(Below) The general officers' M1940 Persian lamb *papaha* winter hat, worn here by a lieutenant-general. This followed Russian and Caucasian folk headgear, and replaced the *budionovka* worn until 1940 by general officers. Generals of some specific services had differently coloured tops – e.g. the Air Force (light blue), NKVD (brick-red), and NKVD Frontier Guards (green) – while generals of Red Army land forces had the red top for all branches. The most expensive examples were made from the fleece of unborn lambs.

Colonels were also permitted to wear the *papaha*, but with the top of greatcoat-coloured grey cloth. The Don Cossacks had a similarly shaped headgear, but with a blue top with crossed red tapes, and the enlisted ranks' cap star from 1936 (see also shorter black *kubanka* on page 116).

(**Above**) *Typical front-line irregularities of uniform: an artillery general gives orders over a field telephone, 1944. The general wears the M1943 officers' spring/autumn topcoat, without regulation collar patches or shoulder boards. His field quality officers' visored cap, to which he has pinned his general officers' everyday cap badge, has a cloth-covered visor and buttons and a cloth chinstrap. The badge is the only exception to his complete anonymity as an otherwise unidentifiable officer.*

His colonel (left) wears some kind of apparently waterproofed enlisted ranks' working gymnastiorka, with concealed buttons and a pre-1943 falling collar. Despite this he chooses to wear a full-colour everyday cap with the black band and scarlet piping of the artillery. His khaki field shoulder boards have lost one of the stars of his rank. Note also the odd size of the shoulder boards – about 5cm (2ins) shorter than they should be.

(*Left*) *By contrast, this Air Force major photographed in the Far East Military District in 1945 has received a pair of shoulder boards for his everyday tunic that protrude about 2ins further over his shoulders than they should. The medal is that for Victory over Japan, 1945. Note also the white collar liner just visible; this was officially an issue item but was more usually home-made.*

'THE EMPIRE FIGHTS BACK' – TSARIST HEROES RAISED FROM OBLIVION

The harnessing of traditional heroes of Tsarist Russian history for the sake of national morale from 1943 onwards was surprisingly complete. In the titles and designs of awards, Lenin and Stalin – the 'fathers' of the Soviet Union and the international Communist movement – appeared only once, on the medal awarded to partisans, and no other heroes of the Soviet period were invoked at all.

Analysis of the whole range of Soviet orders and medals shows that all the decorations established before 1942 featured a range of typically Communist symbols: not only the star and hammer-and-sickle and the red banner, but hydro-electric power stations, industrial workers and peasant women, Red Army men, aircraft and tanks, and slogans extolling the 'unity of the world's proletariat'. All such symbolism disappeared with the new orders established in the second half of the war, to be replaced with Imperial symbols and heroes. Slogans proclaimed the 'Patriotic War' in conscious reference back to the national resistance to Napoleon's invasion of 1812, and were accompanied by the basic military symbolism of rifles and swords; and the names of the orders invoked Russian heroes dating from the Middle Ages to the 19th century – Alexander Nevski, Suvorov, Nachimov, Kmelnitski, Ushakov and Kutuzov.

(Above) This major of artillery wearing the officer's 1943 mundir parade tunic displays on his right breast, above the badge of a Guard unit, three awards of the Order of the Patriotic War and one of Alexander Nevski. More than one award of the Order of the Patriotic War – 'Otechka' – of the same class was so unusual as to be almost unique.

(Left) This major of Militia (police) wears that service's dark parade mundir; dark blue was used by regular Militia and black by Transport and River Militia. Note the double bars of lace on the cuff and similar collar bars, worn by field grade officers – i.e. majors, lieutenant-colonels and colonels. The central, vertical arrangement of his many medals on the double-breasted tunic is interesting; the bottom row was reserved for foreign medals. On his right side two orders and a Guards badge are also pinned on vertically. The use of a field belt with a parade tunic is irregular.

(**Right**) This lieutenant-colonel has dark-coloured shoulder board stripes and matching collar piping, identifying his branch as either the cavalry or the NKVD, both of which used dark blue. Next to his Order of Alexander Nevski (left, top) is an Order of Suvorov 3rd Class, above two Orders of the Red Star, and one of the Patriotic War. The Suvorov was awarded for outstanding organisational skills on the battlefield. It was established in 1942, and its 1st Class (gold, with a red star at the top) was first awarded to Marshal Zhukov for his Stalingrad operations. This was the first wartime order awarded to the USSR's outstanding commander of World War II, although he had already received the Order of Lenin for defeating the Japanese 6th Army on the Mongolian-Manchurian border in 1939.

(**Below**) This lieutenant-colonel's two awards of the Alexander Nevski are even more extraordinary than the multiple Orders of the Patriotic War on page 97; in wartime most of the high orders could be awarded to an individual only once. The most usual exceptions were the Red Star and the Red Banner. The latter could be awarded repeatedly; the most to an individual were seven, the seventh given in 1967. The Order of the Patriotic War came in two classes, pure silver and gold. Note on this mundir the impressive metallic double collar bars of field grade ranks.

(**Below right**) This colonel tactical instructor commanding a military academy displays an Order of Kutuzov, and at the head of his ribboned medals two Orders of the Red Banner. He would therefore seem well qualified for his appointment: the Kutuzov was given to commanders who planned and launched successful large-scale operations at the level of front, army group or army staffs.

PRISONERS OF WAR

PRISONERS OF WAR

(Above & above right) A Soviet prisoner of war, somewhere in occupied Poland in summer 1944, wears a worn and patched gymnastiorka, with home-made bone buttons. All insignia have been stripped off, and he has also lost his belt and boots. The best he can hope for is to be sent back to Germany to be used as forced labour, and he will be extremely lucky if he is given barely enough food and shelter to live through the coming winter – the survival of their 'sub-human' slaves was a matter of supreme indifference to the Nazis.

(Right) This letter card was issued by the Hungarian Red Cross for Hungarian prisoners of war in Soviet camps. It incorporates a tear-off reply card – although a reply could not, of course, be guaranteed.

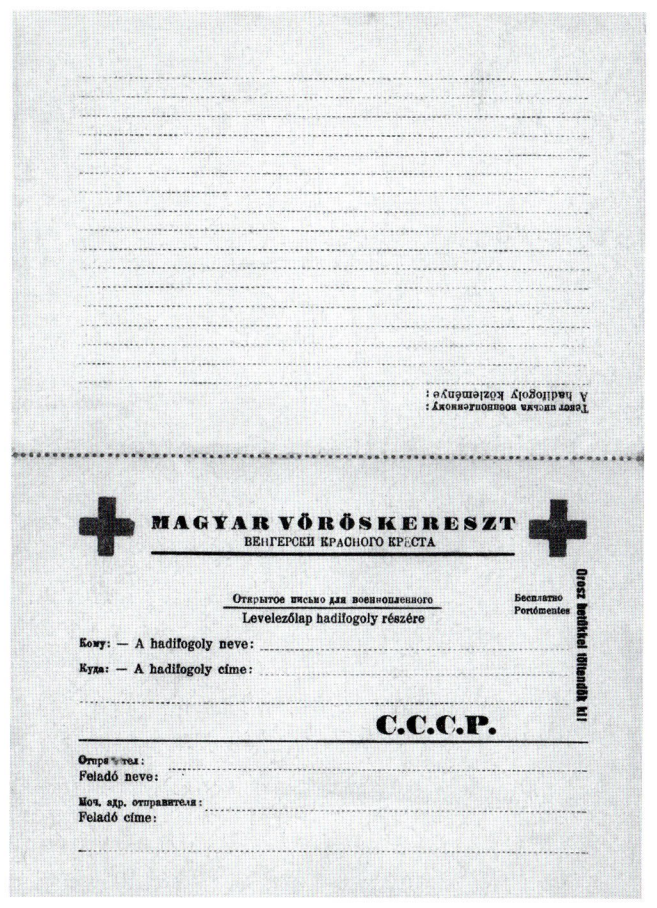

— 99 —

TANK CREWMAN, 1944

(Above) Red Army T-34/85 tanks in the ancient streets of liberated Prague, Czechoslovakia, in spring 1945.

TANK CREWMAN, SUMMER 1944

(Right & opposite) This soldier has the enlisted ranks' M1943 gymnastiorka with standing collar, here unbuttoned since he is off duty. Against regulations, but as a widely tolerated practice in the most prestigious combat branches, he has attached the full-colour everyday quality shoulder boards in black, instead of the regulation soft field boards in khaki, both of which had scarlet piping.

By this date the pre-war tank man's black leather helmet, coat and trousers had virtually disappeared from the battlefield. One-piece overalls were usually issued for wear over the uniform when serving with the vehicle, in grey canvas with a single left breast pocket; some khaki overalls were also supplied by the Western Allies.

Tank troops shared with officers the privilege of carrying a sidearm, by this date normally the TT-30 semi-automatic. The holster slung individually from a diagonal strap, rather than looped to the belt, was an old Russian Imperial tradition still commonly seen in the 1930s. Later only Air Force aircrews and armoured vehicle crews used this arrangement, so that the weapon and sling could be discarded easily without unfastening a belt if the soldier was forced to make an emergency escape from the tight confines of an aircraft or tank. However, internal holster-pockets were also preferred if overalls were available.

(Above right) An example of the classic canvas protective helmet for tank and self-propelled gun crews. Note the ear housings for an intercom system; before 1943 only platoon commanders' tanks had radios at all, and although they were fitted in all T-34/85s, for the first half of the war the crews had no direct communications within the tank, so pre-action briefings were of great importance.

(Right) The stamp on the inside of this helmet flap; the '3' indicates large size. In other kinds of headgear the diameter was marked in centimetres. Buttons, rings and patent fasteners were all widely used for fastening the flaps of tank helmets.

(Opposite) The helmet neck flap could be worn in either the up or down position, depending on weather conditions. Note also the aluminium canteen in its numbered canvas carrier.

TANK CREWMAN, 1944

TANK CREWMAN, 1944

(Opposite) The 7.62mm Tula-Tokarev (TT) M1930 semi-automatic pistol, with an officer's field belt, holster, strap lanyard, eight-round magazine, rounds, and cleaning rod. This efficient weapon – which followed a basic Browning design, but featured Tokarev's innovative feed mechanism – was, with the slightly modified TT-33 model, the standard sidearm for officers and vehicle crews in the second half of the war (although the M1895 Nagant seven-shot revolver was still to be seen). Rounds for the TT and the revolver can be told apart easily, since the latter had the bullet sunk completely inside the cartridge case.

(Above) Compare this tank or tank-destroyer crew helmet with that on page 100. Such variations are commonly found – the canvas was either grey or black and of various weaves; the size of the padded sections varied, as did the fastenings. One reliable indication of use with the T-34 and KV tanks of World War II manufacture is the presence of three front-to-back padded tubes over the top of the skull; post-war helmets for the crews of T-54/55 and later designs have four such tubes.

(Right) The bakelite grip of a TT-30 semi-automatic pistol; note the star surrounded by the abbreviation 'CCCP' – the Cyrillic form of 'SSSR'.

TANK CREWMAN, 1944

(Right) Note the worn-out breeches with unskilful repairs by the wearer. The colour contrast between the khaki shades of the *gymnastiorka* and breeches is also striking, although both would officially be called 'olive'. In wartime, the parts of uniforms worn by individuals were nearly always mixed within a few months of initial issue, and in front line photographs it is hard to find anyone with a blouse and breeches of exactly the same material or showing the same degree of fading from sunlight, dust and washing. Inevitably, one half of the uniform had to be replaced before the other, and under war conditions nobody cared about a smart match.

(Above) The M1940 'recon knife' is usually found stamped by the Tula arsenal with a 'T', or by the Kirov factory at Leningrad with 'ZIK'. The wooden scabbard and the hilt had a poor quality black paint finish. The main purpose of its introduction was to give the front-line soldier a simple, cheap, easy-to-make and easy-to-replace edged weapon and tool, since the old-fashioned cruciform needle bayonet for the Nagant rifle was more or less useless for any other purpose, and the Red Army issued no pocket knife or eating knife. The knife was nominally intended for reconnaissance scouts, but was widely used by other troops.

Note also the cleaning rod in its stowage loops on the front of the TT holster; and the field-baked square loaf. This can be seen represented on the 1944 Excellence badge for 'Excellent Baker'.

(Right) A page from the 'Fighters' Calendar'. The pages for December 1944 in this pocket diary note the 'weak points and effective ways of damaging German Tiger tanks': cupola vision slots, sight aperture in the gun mantlet, pistol port, rear reloading hatch, engine deck, driver's and hull gunner/radio operator's hatches and apertures, as well as road wheels, sprockets and idlers.

In June 1941 the Red Army had enormous numbers of obsolete tanks, manned by poorly trained crews and led by unskilled officers. In six months more than 90 per cent of the 28,000 tanks originally available were lost, to a German Panzer force with only some 3,500 tanks; and although many of the excellent new T-34/76 tanks reached the front in 1942, it was not until well into 1943 that new equipment and the lessons of battle really matured the armoured branch. However, even in 1944–45 the latest T-34/85 had little chance in a one-to-one frontal engagement against the PzKw V Panther or (thankfully much rarer) PzKw VI Tiger; and success in even short range flank attacks on the Tiger usually depended on scarce supplies of the enhanced Soviet BR-365P 85mm armour-piercing shells.

IMPROVISED ITEMS

Shortages of regulation issue items, and the traditional creativity of Russian soldiers, led to the appearance of a wide variety of home-made or improvised pieces of kit during the Great Patriotic War. Only fifty years beforehand most units had still been expected to make their own uniforms at regimental level from supplied bolts of cloth; and even in the 1940s there were stories of newly joined recruits being given material and sent home so that their mothers could make up trousers in their sons' sizes.

(**Above & right**) These are (bottom in each case) a regular issue officer's 'Sam Browne'-style belt, and (top) an improvised version. The government issue example has a one-piece cut-out star buckle, and the belt itself is doubled and sewn for strength. The upper belt has a two-piece buckle with a geometrically incorrect star, and is of a single thickness of leather. The holster for the TT-30 Tokarev pistol is also improvised, apparently cut from some German leather item – probably a map case.

105

MOSIN RIFLES, SOLDIERS' EQUIPMENT & SMALL KIT

MOSIN RIFLES, AND SOLDIERS' EQUIPMENT AND SMALL KIT

(Top to bottom, left to right)

Copy of Red Army field service regulations, 1933.

M1891/30 Mosin-Nagant rifle, with 4× power sniper scope, and cruciform, screwdriver-tipped socket bayonet.

Stripper clip of 5 rounds of 7.62mm ammunition.

Red-covered trade union membership book, between two 1943 leaflets on river-crossing techniques.

M1944 carbine version of Mosin-Nagant, with permanently fixed folding bayonet, and empty stripper clip.

Rifle ammunition pouches, black Naval Infantry issue.

Aluminium canteen in carrier.

Bandages, soap, razor, matches, cigarette lighters, cigarette case, cigarette packet.

M1940 'recon knife'.

Belt, with: canteen, case for sniper scope, various rifle ammunition pouches.

Entrenching tool.

Maxim machine gun feed belt used as cartridge belt, with hand grenade pouch.

Bakelite box for butter or boot grease.

*The immediate differences between the M1891 and M1891/30 Mosin-Nagant rifles, and the M1944 carbine. The earlier Imperial rifle (**above, top; left, bottom; opposite**) had the rear sight mounted in a 'stepped' housing; in the 1930 modification (**above, centre; left, top**) the sight mounting is of a 'wave' shape. The shortened 1944 carbine (**above, bottom**) differed both in its length and in the bayonet. The latter was of the same basic design but slightly shortened, and was permanently fixed to fold back down the right hand side of the weapon. The earlier long socket bayonets were not issued in scabbards, and caused many accidental injuries. When the M1930 bayonet was carried reversed, i.e. pointing backwards down the barrel, it was also forever getting snagged in equipment.*

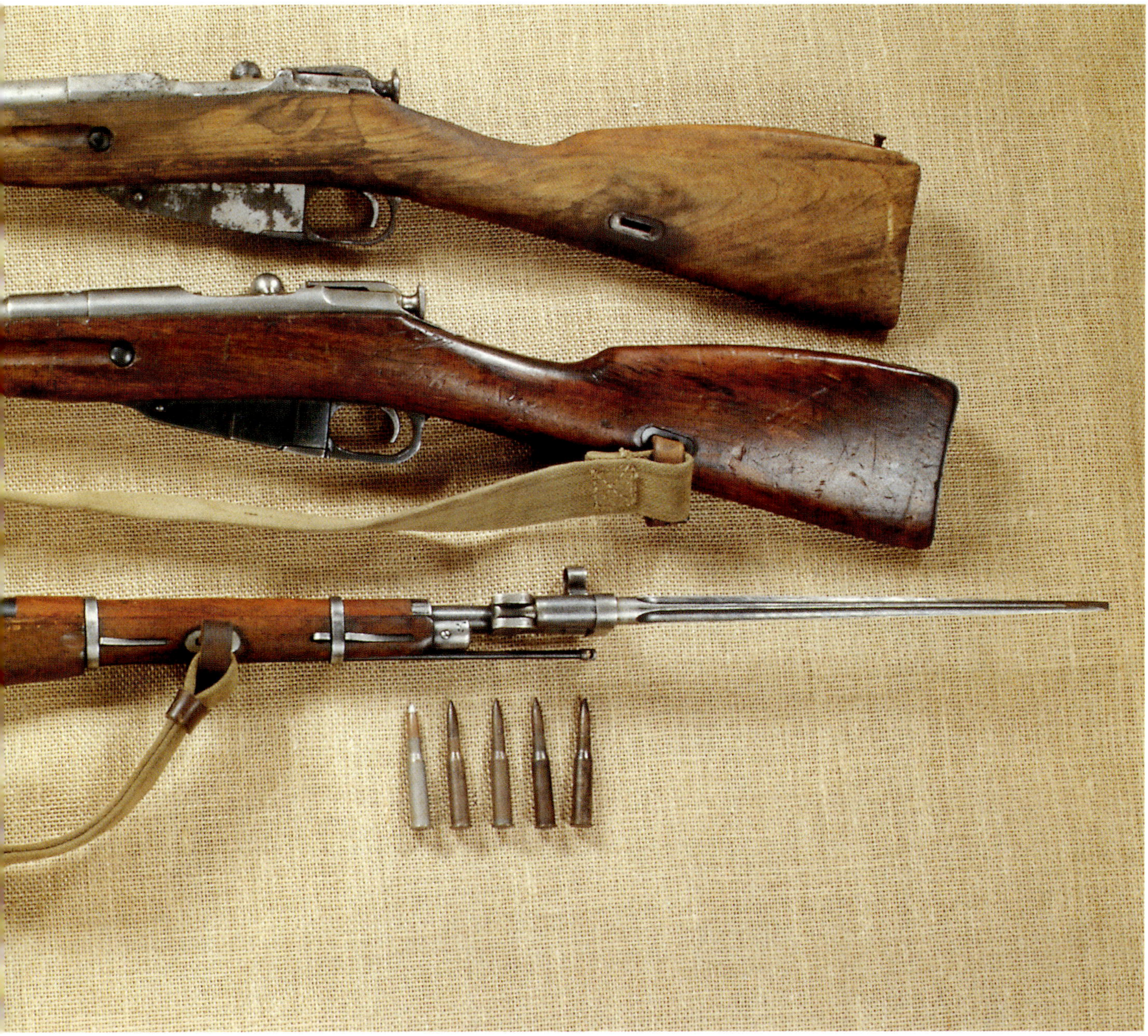

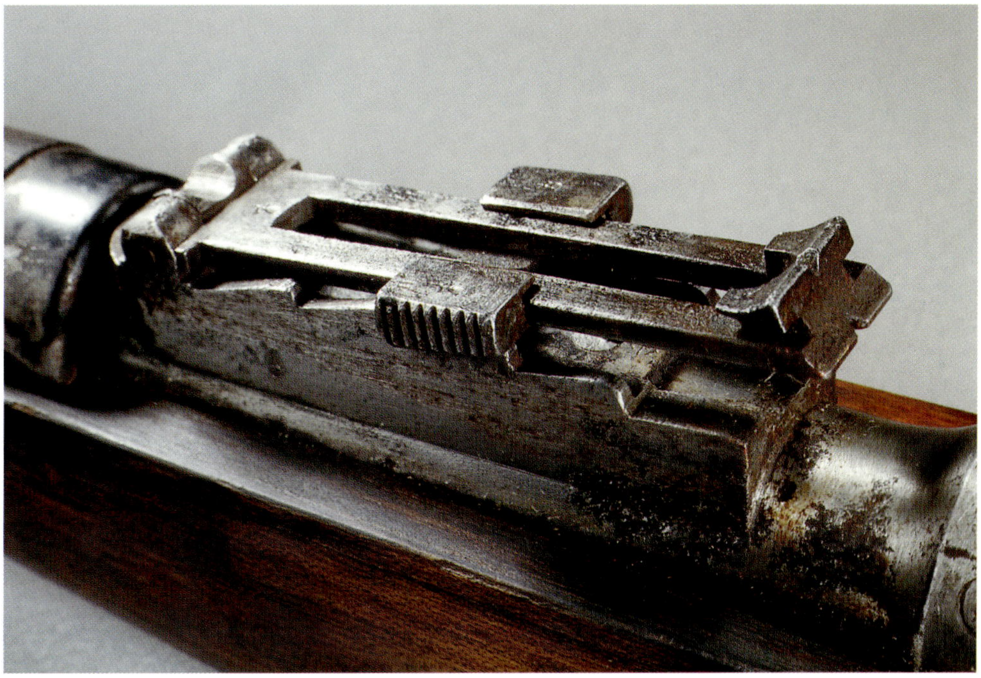

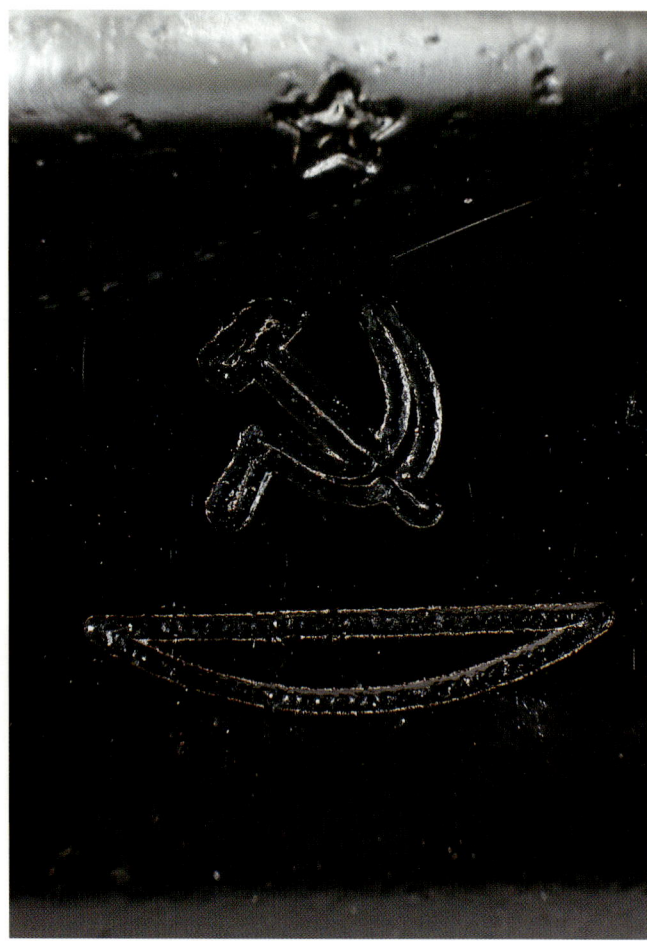

(Above) *Adjustment drums and factory stamps on a 4× power sniper scope made in 1938 – note the 'lens' symbol beneath the hammer-and-sickle. The Red Army took sharpshooting seriously in the 1930s, and by 1942 the ordnance factories were selecting particularly accurate M1891/30 rifles from the production runs for fitting with telescopic sights at a rate of some 53,000 per year. The original model of this 4× scope was an imported Carl Zeiss product designated the PT. Imports ceased in 1935, and thereafter a Soviet copy was made under the designation VP or PEM – from the date, this must be the model depicted. From 1940 this equipment began to be replaced by the lighter and handier 3.5× PU sight, mounted with a single rear clamp, although all three types were to be seen in simultaneous use throughout the war; the 4× scope was preferred by many veterans, giving good accuracy out to about 800 metres.*

Soviet propaganda made a great deal of the skill of their snipers, and particularly – for obvious reasons – of the women; in the desperate days of 1941 many 'snipers' were sent to the front too hastily trained to really justify that term, although there was a generally high level of marksmanship in those provincial formations recruited partly from among rural hunters. Later on there is no doubt that snipers made a serious contribution, and this was confirmed by German records. The Central Women's Sniper School alone graduated more than 1,000 trainees during the war, who between them were officially credited with shooting about 12,000 of the enemy (see **SUM**, page 38). Six women snipers received the gold star of Heroine of the Soviet Union; the highest number of kills officially credited to an individual was the 309 to Major Lyudmila Mikhailovna Pavlichenko.

(Left) *A young krasnoarmeyets with his Mosin-Nagant M1891/30 slung, passing a dead enemy frozen in the snow. He wears the conventional* ushanka *and* shinel, *with* valenki *felt overboots. Compared with that of his German opponents, the personal equipment of the Soviet soldier was often simple, elderly and unsophisticated; but – like the peasant soldier himself – it was sturdy, available in huge numbers, and served its purpose well.*

OFFICERS' VISORED CAPS

(Left) *Full-colour everyday/parade cap of an officer of armoured troops, probably of pre-war manufacture. The band and piping are in black velvet and scarlet respectively, colours shared with the artillery; but the crown is in steel-grey rather than khaki – the distinction introduced in the 1935 regulations for the uniforms of this prestigious arm of service.*

Note the standard enamelled star badge, black patent leather chinstrap and gilt buttons. The visor is of the early shape seen also in the photograph below.

(Below) *A similar cap for an officer of the NKVD. The band should be described as brick-red, and the slightly differing piping to the cornflower-blue crown as the raspberry-red of rifles troops. This early visor shape was called 'lopata', 'entrenching spade', a semi-squared outline that dates back to the Russo-Japanese war of 1904–05.*

OFFICERS' VISORED CAPS

(Left) A dark blue and scarlet Militia officer's cap, with the standard red star badge ordered in 1939, although the more ornate former design featuring the coat of arms was also used throughout the war. The same colours were used for the Cossack cap.

(Below) An officer's cap of either the Red Army's technical or transport branches, which shared a black band and light blue piping.

— 112 —

OFFICERS' VISORED CAPS

(Left) This black band and duller blue piping identify the caps worn by chemical troops and some engineers.

(Right) Artillery Senior Sergeant Ivashin, 1944, displaying the supreme decorations of the gold star of a Hero of the Soviet Union and the Order of Lenin. Note the field quality cap, entirely in plain khaki, with a cloth chinstrap and cloth-covered visor. His khaki field shoulder boards have red piping, broad red rank loops, and the branch insignia. His beard, and (visible in the original uncropped print) a personal edged weapon – a 'Finnish'-type hunting knife with a high quality bone grip – give him a more individualistic appearance than many senior commanders. While moustaches were allowed, and popular, beards were officially permitted only to hide a facial injury.

(Left) Officers' visored field dress cap in khaki. Various qualities and variations had been in use since the mid-1920s; the first issues had pairs of small ventilators low on the crown sides. Note the cloth-covered buttons but patent leather chinstrap and olive plastic visor of this particular model, in contrast to Ivashin's cap above. Some individuals discarded the cap badge to further reduce visibility.

113

THE NKVD

The different organs of the NKVD played an important, if sometimes sinister role in the conduct of the war by Stalin's regime. The straightforward part played by the Frontier Guards in the first defensive battles of June 1941 has already been mentioned; they already had some combat experience, for instance in the Khalkin Gol campaign against the Japanese incursion into Mongolia in 1939.

The security units of the NKVD were charged with combating defeatism and maintaining public order, sometimes close to the front line, as in the winter of 1941/42 when the approach of the Wehrmacht caused serious public panic. Throughout the USSR the NKVD were responsible for the security of power stations, strategically important factories, and stocks of materials, goods and food. They provided escorts for road, waterway and rail transport convoys. NKVD troops guarded the real or supposed 'internal enemies' of the regime in prisons and GULAG camps, and both interrogated and later guarded enemy prisoners of war. Their responsibilities were so widespread that they embraced both the Kremlin Guard and the country's fire brigades.

As the guardians of state security the NKVD were also naturally responsible for intelligence and to a lesser extent counter-intelligence; but the Red Army also had its own well-known counter-intelligence department, SMERSh. This latter was responsible for tasks including monitoring German radio traffic, coding and deciphering, maintaining the security of the front lines, questioning prisoners, and hunting for suspected enemy agents within the Red Army (particularly among high-ranking personnel).

(Right) An NKVD sergeant, 240th Rifles Brigade, 1943, identified by field-type shoulder boards with everyday gold rank stripes and painted numbers. The small 20mm Cyrillic 'B' after the numerals indicates that this is a brigade number; if the character was the same size – 32mm – as the numerals, it indicated an Air Force bomber regiment. Note the patch breast pockets on the M1943 gymnastiorka, usually a distinction worn by enlisted ranks only of the NKVD.

(Left) A German prisoner of war is questioned by an artillery major (centre) and senior lieutenant of a Guards unit; it is pure coincidence that on this print the shadows already seem to be closing around the prisoner (whose belt has already been confiscated, probably for re-use by a Soviet soldier). Both officers wear khaki field-quality caps with cloth chinstraps and cloth-covered peaks. Unlike the major, the senior lieutenant displays no arm-of-service insignia; he is unidentifiable, and his lack of combat decorations might suggest Army counter-intelligence? The major wears the everyday M1943 kitel standing-collar tunic with full orders and medals – not very commonly seen in combat zones. Note that he has the orders of Alexander Nevski, the Patriotic War, and a first model Red Banner worn without a ribbon next to a city defence medal. Before suspension ribbons were introduced all screw-back orders (like the Red Star) were supposed to be placed on the right side.

(**Right**) *Two leather-coated NKVD commanders, 1943, flanking a Red Army rifles officer in a long, bulky greatcoat. While the infantry officer has the new regulation coat collar patches in raspberry-red with a single large button, the other two figures have irregular uniforms. The left-hand man has a field-quality cap without a badge, and no shoulder boards. The man on the right has an earlier-style leather coat with a deep falling collar without insignia. His everyday visored cap, again without a badge, has a brick-red band and khaki crown – a sign of NKVD Internal Forces personnel, probably from the Fourth Directorate responsible for control 'Close Behind the Front Lines'. Set up in the spring of 1943, this directorate freely applied the sanction known in a grim soldiers' joke as 'Paragraph 7.62' of the basic law – the calibre of the state's normal response to suspected or actual desertion. Under the coat note the gymnastiorka of late 1920s style with a deep falling collar, from which any rank patches have been removed.*

It was common for NKVD personnel, both in the war zones and far behind the lines, to hide their ranks, and to wear civilian-style coats with anonymous plastic or bone buttons. The aim was to bolster their menacing mystique, confusing those they dealt with as to their exact status and authority.

(**Below**) *NKVD troops, 1944. Just visible on the shoulder boards of the two central sitting figures is the 'UVV' cypher of the Ukraine Internal Troops. This is painted on to the cloth, and no regimental numbers are displayed. These men have a variety of different belts, with either one- or two-claw frame buckles or the cut-out officers' star. Shiny collar buttons, like cap badges, were sometimes removed in the front lines.*

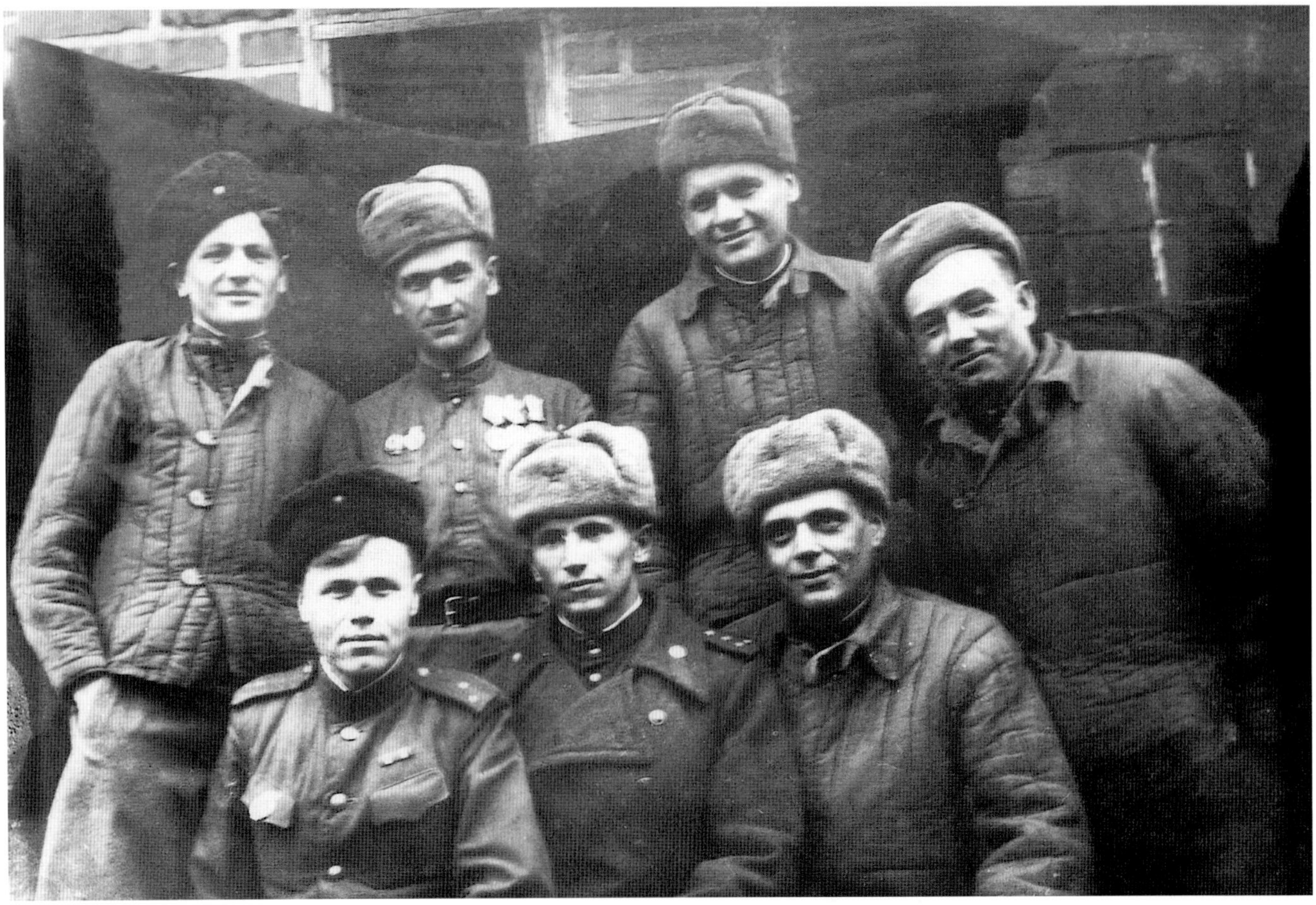

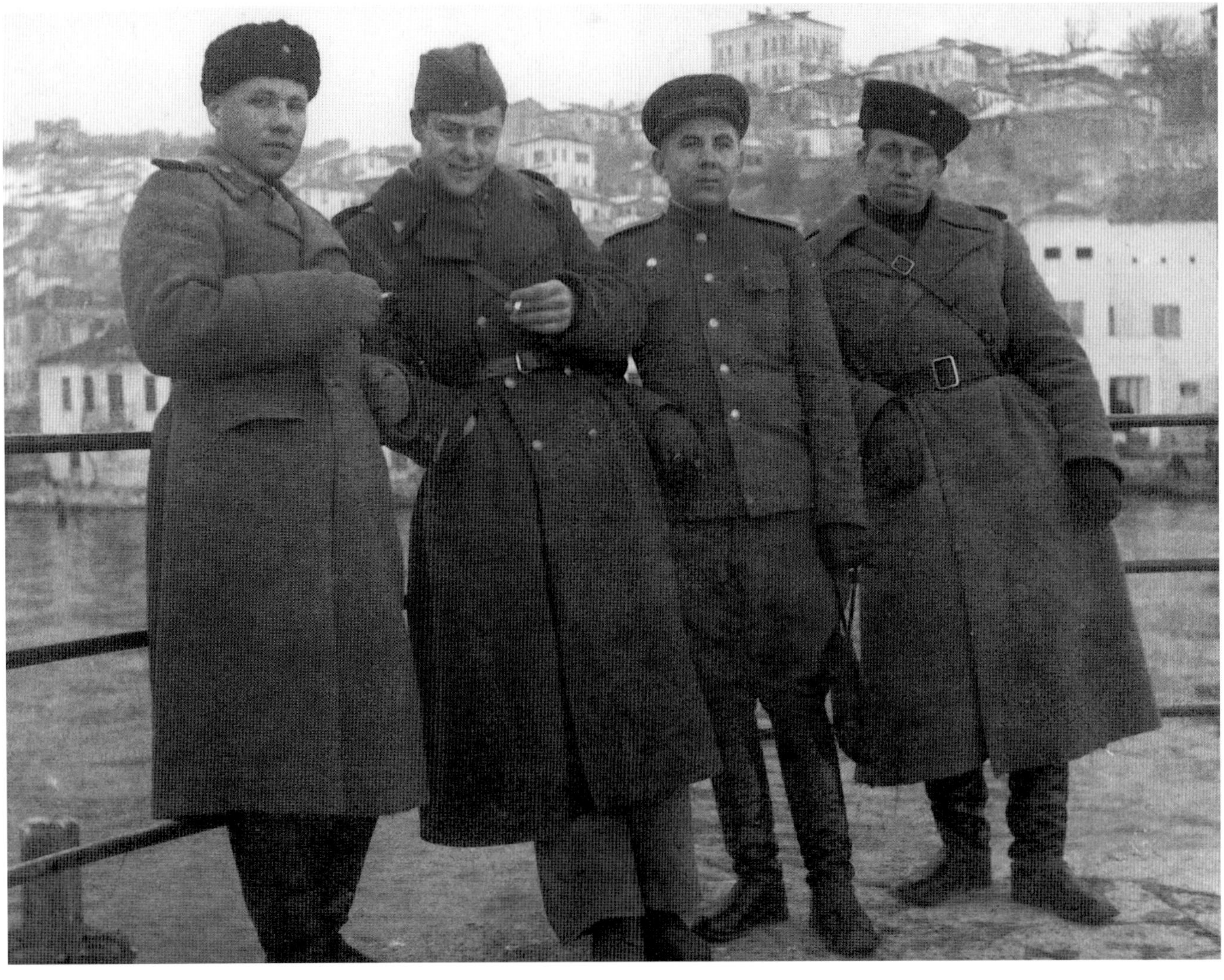

(**Opposite**) *Two groups of officers in winter dress; but are they NKVD, Red Army cavalry, or Militia? The puzzle lies in the difficulty of distinguishing in monochrome photographs between two types of similar fleece hats, the* kubanka *and the* finka.

Shallow kubanka *hats in dark fleece (taking their name from the Kuban Cossack host) were used by Cossack cavalry troopers, but also by NKVD troops and Militia. For the cavalry the fleece was black and the cloth tops cornflower-blue, with crossed tapes or piping in yellow or red; after the 1943 reforms such caps without this cruciform decoration were also made for the NKVD.*

The shapka-finka *was the winter hat for the Militia between 1940 and 1943; it resembled the* kubanka, *but was of dark brown fleece with a midnight-blue top; it also had the fleece band made in two parts so that the rear could be folded up or down – unlike the* kubanka. *This folding rear flap was a simple rectangle, and the* finka *lacked the two longer fold-up/tie-down ear flaps of the* shapka-ushanka *– the standard Red Army winter cap from 1941–42.*

Since both NKVD and Cossacks in practice used a mixture of kubankas *and* shapka-ushankas, *it is therefore unclear whether the left-hand officers in the upper photograph, and the flanking officers in the lower, are from the NKVD or the Cossack cavalry. Incidentally, in the lower photo they are standing on the famous bridge at Mostar in Bosnia, with (second left) a Yugoslavian partisan officer wearing triangular rank insignia on his greatcoat collar.*

(**Above**) *The short Persian lamb* kubanka *hat in black or dark grey, with crossed tape stripes or piping on the cloth top, was a distinction of the Cossacks, and they often wore it proudly all year round, not only in winter. The traditional colour combinations were blue, crossed red, for Don Cossacks; red, crossed black, for Kuban Cossacks; and light blue, crossed yellow, for Terek (Caucasian) Cossacks. In wartime, however, these exact distinctions were not always observed; and anyway, the Steppe Cossack hosts – of which the Don was only the most prominent – had used in Tsarist times a variety of combinations of dark and light blues and reds, yellow and even green.*

(**Left**) *Lieutenant-colonel of the NKVD, c.1944, in the blue and red visored cap, and wearing the M1943 officers' spring/autumn topcoat. This double-breasted garment, closed with two rows of three buttons, was made of fairly lightweight material, and bore no NKVD sleeve patches or officers' cuff piping. It does display the red collar patches piped in dark blue, as introduced for the greatcoat in February 1943 NKVD uniform regulations. Note one small detail – the rank stars on his shoulder boards are not, as was usual, pinned to the two field officers' dark blue rank stripes, but to the gold lace outside them.*

NKVD COMMANDER

(*Right & opposite*) *Unusual views of an NKVD officer, which might be from any summer of the war, since without his gymnastiorka or tunic the rank insignia system could be either pre- or post-February 1943. He wears a light linen collarless undershirt; this followed the cut of the gymnastiorka, and drawers of the same material followed that of the breeches. The custom of wearing blue sharovary breeches in the field ceased generally throughout the Red Army during the war, as it was a telltale sign to enemy marksmen that this was a high-value target. The NKVD, less often in the presence of the enemy, frequently retained them, since their cornflower-blue matched that of the everyday visored cap and the rank stripes on the shoulder boards; like the cap, the breeches were piped at the seams with the raspberry-red of Red Army rifle troops. Note the braces; in wartime these were used to support all riding-cut breeches, in khaki or blue, and narrow belts were only substituted in the post-war period.*

This commander, on some behind-the-lines security duty, holds the usual TT M1930 semi-automatic, with its leather lanyard strap unfastened from his belt and hanging free.

(*Opposite, inset*) *Short 7.62mm × 25mm rimless ammunition for the TT pistol and PPSh/PPS sub-machine guns. The headstrap shows the date for 1944 and '3' identifying the factory.*

NKVD COMMANDERS

SHOULDER BOARDS, NKVD REGULATIONS, FEBRUARY 1943

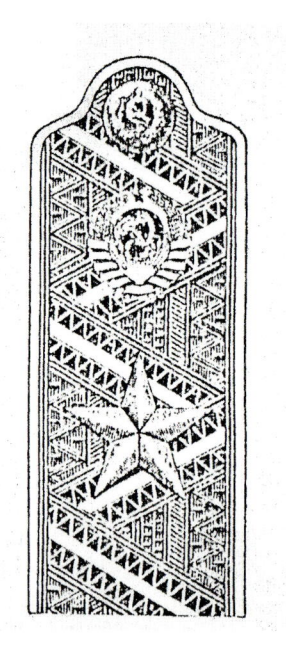

Shortly after the Red Army reform regulations of Prikaz 25 on 15 January 1943, the NKVD's Prikaz 126 of 18 February followed suit in discontinuing the collar patch rank system and fall-collar garments. Standing-collar Imperial-type gymnastiorkas and tunics were reinstated, complete with shoulder boards. However, the first NKVD regulations illustrate shoulder boards of a most unusual shape, which we reproduce on these pages. After the initial production run they were cancelled, and replaced with boards of the classic shape, with the button end clipped in three straight edges.

NKVD CAPTAIN, 1943

This officer follows the security service's new uniform regulations of 18 February 1943, which in general terms matched those of the Red Army issued the previous month. He wears the full colour everyday cap in cornflower-blue with red band and piping. Although it is not clear in this photograph, there is blue piping around the collar and cuff tops of the stand-collar kitel tunic in dark khaki. The everyday shoulder boards in gold lace have blue edging and rank stripes, and the four gold stars of his rank. This tunic would be worn with the red-piped dark blue breeches, or unpiped khaki, depending on location and duty.

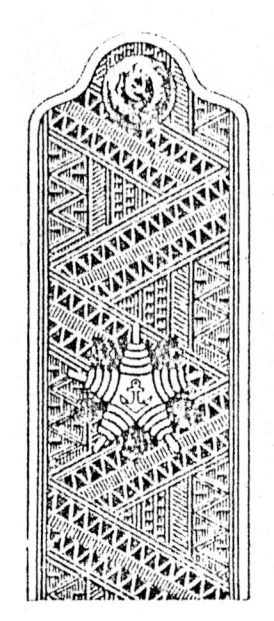

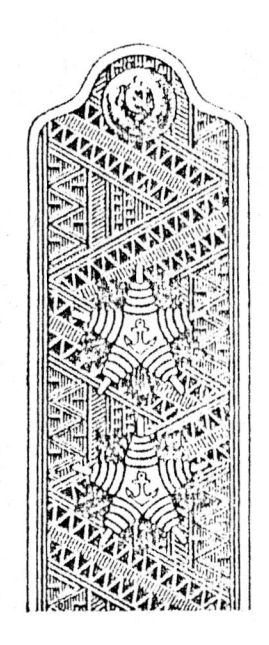

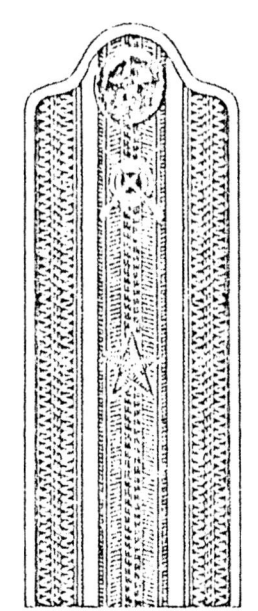

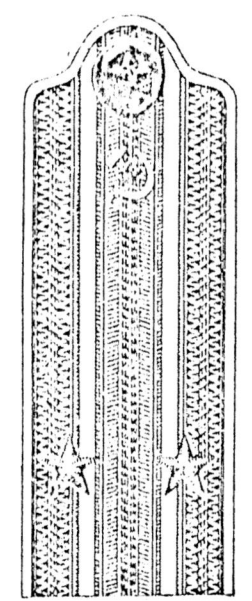

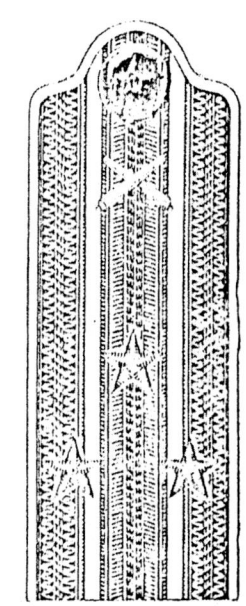

(Opposite top right) General commissar – this rank was equivalent to marshal of the Soviet Union, and was borne only by Lavrenti Beria. Gold embroidered lace, cornflower-blue piping, silver embroidered star, silver and gold embroidered arms of the USSR; gilt button with same arms. The zig-zag lace pattern was a typical late 19th century feature for generals and marshals in many armies.

(Above left) Rear admiral and vice admiral, NKVD Seagoing Frontier Guards. (The NKVD had not only its own integral cavalry, armoured, artillery, and engineer units, but also naval and air branches – even its own veterinary service.) Gold lace, piped in the green of the Frontier Guards; stars with anchors, and coat-of-arms buttons as for general officers. While general officer equivalents of the NKVD Frontier and Internal Troops and some other branches (e.g. the legal department) kept Army-style generals' rank titles, those of the NKVD central organs and Militia bore the titles of commissar 1st, 2nd and 3rd ranks.

(Above centre & right) Major, with old-style rifles insignia – this was soon discontinued, and thereafter NKVD rifle troops used no branch insignia; lieutenant-colonel, NKVD supply corps; colonel, NKVD Internal Troops artillery.

(Below) NKVD collar and cuff insignia for senior ranks' parade tunics. These were very similar to Imperial patterns, in rich gold and silver embroidery. (Below left) General Commissar Beria; (below right) other commissars of the three ranks equivalent to general officers.

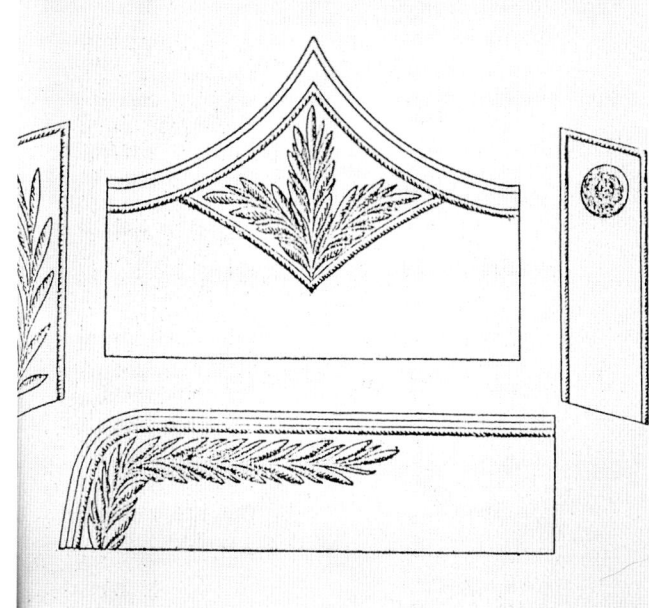

SELF-PROPELLED GUN CREWMAN, 1945

THE ADVANCE TO BERLIN, SUMMER 1944–SPRING 1945

SELF-PROPELLED GUN CREWMAN, 1945

This dismounted member of the crew of one of the SU self-propelled guns in the integral artillery unit of a mechanised rifle brigade, who has taken to the street with the DT machine gun dismounted from his perhaps damaged or broken-down vehicle, wears typical winter dress for armoured troops in the last months of the war.

The padded helmet is of the standard pattern for all armoured vehicle crews. Note that his double-breasted coat is of heavy canvas and thickly lined, but does not have the visible quilting seams of the classic telogreika. *On its fall collar are displayed the everyday greatcoat collar patches of the 1943 regulations – here in infantry raspberry-red piped black, not the scarlet-piped black of artillery. Although the shoulders have fixing loops for shoulder boards, this soldier chooses not to wear them – they were liable to snag on the many obstacles inside the cramped fighting compartment of an armoured vehicle, and for those who had no rank to display they were pointless. Note the long, lambskin-lined gauntlet gloves of soft leather, typical for armoured troops and sometimes also worn by other vehicle crews, dispatch riders, etc. These were originally issued only for drivers, and it was strictly forbidden to use them for other purposes such as maintenance and repair work.*

(Left) Head stamps on a round of 7.62mm ammunition, common to the Mosin rifles and DP and DT light machine guns. Apart from the antiquated M1895 revolver, just two types of 7.62mm cartridges – for rifles/machine guns, and pistols/submachine guns – satisfied all the Red Army's needs for small arms ammunition throughout the war, thus greatly simplifying logistics. This particular round was produced in 1938 – the year of the great purges, when Stalin's paranoia sent many Red Army commanders to face NKVD firing squads on trumped-up charges.

(Above) Details of the DT machine gun. The adjustable, folding skeleton shoulder stock has a leather pad. The small drum magazines still took 60 rounds; though specially designed to fit more easily in the confines of the hull of an armoured fighting vehicle (where large numbers could therefore be stowed), they were also convenient for infantry engaged in the urban fighting which characterised the latter part of the war. The optical sight (top) is that which fitted into the aperture in the ball mounting for the gun in the front hull of e.g. the T-34 tank, moving with the gun and 'zeroed' to it. The bipod legs and the alternative front sight, for dismounted use, were made as a single assembly; when the gun was mounted in the vehicle they were replaced by another fixture (seen here beneath the barrel) and the optical sight.

Note also the details of the padded helmet, goggles, and winter gauntlets.

DT & DP MACHINE GUNS

(*Above*) Comparison between the compact DT, and (above it) the DP – Russia's most widely used infantry light machine gun of the war (DT stands for 'Degtyarev, Tank' and DP for 'Degtyarev, Pulemet'). The two weapons have the same basic mechanism, but the latter has a wooden stock and an air-cooling sleeve around the barrel, and took big, shallow 47-round dish magazines. Here the DT's flash suppressor at the muzzle is in the reversed position, to shorten the length for transport or stowage (see right).

It is notable that in the second half of the war Axis ammunition boxes were often marked with reminders to 'be sparing with ammunition', while the Red Army's wooden and metal ammo cases sometimes bore exhortations to do exactly the opposite.

Machine gun handling in snow conditions – recommended techniques for transport and use of guns and ammunition with a snow sled, from the 1941 winter warfare manual. The old belt-fed, water-cooled M1910 Maxim, shrouded under a cover, is shown (right) – it was still in production, with minor modifications, throughout the Great Patriotic War. The DP (below) first appeared in 1926. A wartime modification, the DPM, can be recognized by a tube protruding from the rear of the receiver to hold the operating spring (the original DP had it coiled around the piston rod under the barrel, which could cause a hot gun to malfunction).

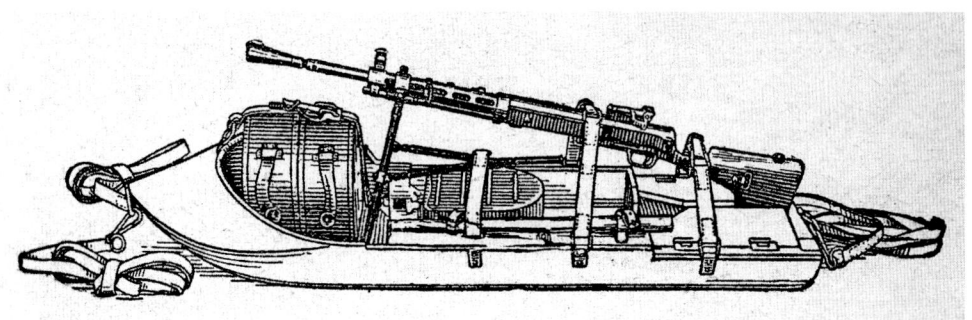

(Right) These drawings show the unsuccessful Goryunov DS of 1939, a heavier belt-fed version of the DP with new cooling fins round the barrel, spade grips and a thumb trigger. It could be mounted on a tripod for sustained fire, and was often fitted with the same steel shield as the Maxim – machine gun crews were always priority targets.

JUNIOR LIEUTENANT, ENGINEERS, SPRING 1945

A typical field uniform for a junior officer in the final weeks of the war: everyday cap, officer's gymnastiorka with field quality shoulder boards, khaki breeches, and fine leather boots. As a field or camouflage engineer the main differences are the black band and dull blue piping on his cap, the black edging to his shoulder boards, and the matching piping – unusual at this date – on his breeches. As one of the most important roles of engineers involved working with timber, the traditional everyday shoulder board emblem was crossed axes.

*(**Below**) Note the 'recon knife' – carried simply as a general purpose tool – and the black piping to the breeches.*

MAJOR, VETERINARY SERVICE, 1945

This officer wears the parade tunic – mundir – introduced by the January 1943 regulations. It differs from the everyday kitel *in having no external pocket flaps; in the more extensive piping, down the front edge; in having piped, two-button false pocket flaps flanking the central rear vent; and in the metallic lace bars on collar patches and cuffs. It is worn with the everyday full-coloured cap and shoulder boards, and cornflower-blue* sharovary *piped in scarlet.*

The veterinary service was classed as a non-combatant branch, and so wore silver lace – though note (opposite) the gold zig-zag decoration on the silver bars on the collar patches. These latter are in the branch's dark green distinguishing colour, like the cap band. The veterinaries used the same emblem as the medical service on their silver shoulder boards, which had scarlet edging and rank stripes and silver stars. Note the double cuff bars, identifying field-grade officers, like those on the collar patches and the double rank stripes on the shoulder boards of majors, lieutenant-colonels and colonels. The order worn on his right breast is that of the Patriotic War; the medal on his left breast is for the Defence of Stalingrad.

In Red Army slang veterinaries were 'dog-doctors'. Another nickname still to be heard was 'Frantsuz' for an interpreter – 'Frenchman', dating back to the Napoleonic wars, when it was used of a French-speaker serving with the unit.

MAJOR, VETERINARY SERVICE, 1945

VETERINARY SERVICE

(Left) *Veterinary officer's visored cap. These are sometimes mistaken by collectors for those of the more glamorous NKVD Frontier Guards. The veterinaries had this deep green band, a khaki crown and scarlet piping; the Frontier Troops, a brighter green crown, midnight-blue band, and raspberry-red piping.*

(Right) *A manual illustration of a pack horse loaded with a mortar.*

Horses were an important part of the transport of both sides on the Eastern Front, in both the pack and the draft roles, and large numbers of veterinaries were necessary to keep them fit for service. Neither the German nor the Soviet supply corps was fully motorised; armoured fighting vehicles had priority in the industrial effort, and the shortages of 'soft-skin' trucks and fuel to run them were compounded by the USSR's primitive dirt roads, which became hardly usable by wheeled transport in the spring thaw and autumn rains. Horsed cavalry also had a genuine combat role until the end of the war, for the same reasons.

(Below) *Large dogs were also pressed into military service in winter, hauling casualties on special sleds, and supplies and munitions in sleds and small boats.*

— 130 —

THE FLAG OF VICTORY:
BERLIN, 1 MAY 1945

On that day Sgts Yegorov and Kantaria and Red Army photographer Yevgeny Khaldei ran up to the roof of the Reichstag and raised this flag (the figures at upper right are statues along the edge of the roof). It was a re-enactment: the first flag was in fact raised at 10.50pm on the night of 30 April. Khaldei took a number of images that differed in small details; this print – not hitherto published, and autographed by the photographer – differs from that which appeared on the front page of Pravda in the positions of the tanks and trucks moving in the street at lower left.

Note, incidentally, the hastily painted white ring around the T-34/85 turret top and the cross on its top surface – the Red Army recognition sign for the battle of Berlin. It was badly needed – there were many incidents of 'friendly fire' from both aircraft and ground forces in the confused street fighting of the last three weeks. The German capital finally fell to Marshal Zhukov's and Marshal Koniev's army groups on 2 May, and Germany surrendered less than a week later. From all causes, between 16 April and 8 May 1945 the capture of Berlin cost the Red Army more than 100,000 killed and more than 250,000 wounded.

VICTORY

THE GUNS FALL SILENT: MAY 1945

(Opposite, top) Junior officers and soldiers of an infantry unit celebrate final victory with songs and traditional dances; the accordion was the most popular instrument among Red Army soldiers. The left-hand dancer, with a captured German triple rifle ammunition pouch on his belt, is an NCO, wearing a full-colour everyday visored cap. Behind him is a very young boy-soldier wearing a Wehrmacht belt.

(Opposite, below) The final destination of a four-year journey, travelled at an incalculable cost in lives: the Berlin Reichstag. The burnt-out shell of the German parliament building, captured on the evening of 30 April – the day when Hitler committed suicide in his nearby bunker – became a symbol of the destruction of Berlin and of the entire Third Reich. Note the surfaces of the walls and pillars – after the fighting ceased the Reichstag became the canvas for what may have been the greatest collection of graffiti in the world, since every Soviet soldier wanted to leave a sign of his part in final victory.

Note standing officer at front left: he wears an Allied sheepskin flying jacket.

Demobilisation
This photograph was taken for insertion in the young Red Army veteran's personal dossier when he became a reservist, just before he resumed civilian life after the war. The garment is probably an NCO's everyday kitel *tunic; it shows heavy wear and tear. The shoulder boards showing his rank have been removed – who knows what rank he will have if and when he is recalled to the ranks? – as has the coloured piping round the collar, which cannot be fastened over a bulky civilian sweater. But he still wears his Order of the Red Star on his worn-out khaki jacket, and his eyes still show unmistakably the strain of what he has endured. The simple fact that he is going home makes him a very lucky man.*

TRAFFIC REGULATOR, BERLIN, 1945

TRAFFIC REGULATOR, BERLIN, MAY 1945

(*Opposite & right*) This woman senior sergeant wears the regulation khaki female uniform of *gymnastiorka* buttoned from right to left, khaki skirt, boots, and a dark blue beret, and holds red and yellow traffic direction flags. At the outbreak of war dark blue skirts had been issued, but in combat zones they were soon replaced with khaki, for the same reason that officers discarded their blue breeches. The male-issue *gymnastiorka*, buttoning in the opposite direction, was often worn by women for lack of supplies of the correct type. The khaki field shoulder boards bear the usual broad transverse stripe or loop of senior sergeant. Their scarlet piping was used by artillery and armoured troops; traffic regulation and motorcycle units often formed part of the services of tank 'armies' (in Western parlance, army corps).

There are two signs that this woman has only recently arrived in occupied Berlin from the collapsed Finnish 'Karelian' Front. One, obviously, is the medal for Defence of the Soviet Polar Region, awarded from May 1941. The other is the small white belt pouch, originally made for Mosin ammunition clips when used with white camouflage garments.

(*Below & below right*) Female headdress. Berets were introduced for female personnel of all ranks in dark blue (officially the same cornflower-blue as for *sharovary* and NKVD caps) from August 1941. Due to shortages, at a period when the front was collapsing and German forces were overrunning Western Russia, it was often replaced with the enlisted ranks' khaki *pilotka* – here, an example in dark brown heavyweight woollen cloth.

DOCUMENTS AND EPHEMERA

(Opposite, top) A commander's documents and awards; still kept together 60 years after the war, these allow us to trace the officer's career. Note the stars, buttons and artillery emblem from his long-lost shoulder boards. Profession Books record his studies in military engineering in the 1930s. The small Coupon Book for Order Bearers shows his entitlement, as a recipient of an Order, to some 15 roubles' worth of extra rations each month. His Paybook reveals that from his monthly salary of 500–725 roubles he drew only about 100 roubles, the rest being sent home direct to his family. The early Order Book includes a list of the privileges he – and his family, if he is killed – enjoy as a recipient of the Order of the Red Star: e.g., 50 per cent off the rent of his flat (for other possible benefits see KSSUM, page 105). From his Equipment Book we can see that he was sent to the front with a pilotka, an ushanka, a gymnastiorka, a wool pullover, a shinel, breeches, two sets of underwear, a pair of boots, and a Finnish-type knife. No belt, holster or gloves are listed; no felt overboots, no canteen, helmet, backpack, gasmask bag, map case or compass – and no weapon.... Sometimes soldiers and officers alike had to scavenge the battlefield for necessary items of equipment, or barter for them with cigarettes.

The medals here are for the Defence of Stalingrad (silver, narrow red stripe); Liberation of Konigsberg (black stripes on turquoise – here, very faded); and Victory over Germany (in the old Romanov colours of orange and black).

(Opposite, below) A soldier's journey, traced in Gramota certificates. While campaign medals were distributed for participation in the defence, and later the liberation or occupation of particular cities, in most cases deserving soldiers received only certificates to mark their service. Here we can follow the route of a captain in the Red Army from the summer 1944 battles which smashed the Wehrmacht's Army Group Centre, all the way to Berlin, by the dates of the Orders of the Day issued by Comrade Marshal of the Soviet Union Stalin:

20 June 1944 – crossing of the River Bug into Poland.
16 January 1945 – liberation of Radom, Poland; and crossing of the River Vistula south of Warsaw. The two certificates are dated on the same day, although the actual engagements probably took place on separate days.
19 January 1945 – liberation of Lodz, Poland.
31 January 1945 – entry into Brandenburg province.

The central, coloured certificate is for 2 May 1945 – the capture of Berlin.

(Below) Komsomol membership cards, c.1941. The Soviet system relied upon groups and mass organisations to submerge and control the individual. 'Free' time was taken up by October groups for toddlers, then Young Pioneer groups for older children; the Komsomol was the Party youth organisation, and the preliminary to adult Communist Party membership. Gradually everyone acquired obligations for sports, Red Cross and chemical defence training, amateur dramatic or reading groups, voluntary work weekends, and trade union activities. Most of the Red Army's manpower under the age of 25 came from the Komsomol, and were extolled in propaganda as examples of heroism and self-sacrifice. Komsomol membership booklets were in two languages in non-Russian republics; those pictured are in Russian–Ukrainian and Russian–Armenian. All organisations and workplaces displayed their collective awards; the Komsomol was awarded both military and civilian ('Labour') Orders of the Red Banner for parallel outstanding activities in war and peace. The decoration is an example of the actual Order of the Red Banner for Labour, instituted in 1938.

(*Above*) Examples of field post letters. As in all the combatant armies, strict censorship regulations limited what a soldier could write in his letters home. It was forbidden to mention any details of his unit, its type or its weapons; his location, or indeed any geographical names – such as rivers crossed or towns passed through; journeys made, or means of transport; any military operations; or the ranks or functions of any of his comrades. Soldiers were thus restricted to the most basic messages about their wellbeing – but in practice, such reassurance was probably all that most families wanted. In one of these letters a soldier mentions that he has received the Order of Glory 3rd Class (pictured).

(*Opposite, top*) Stalin's selected speeches, in a German translation for prisoners of war, 1943. This rare pocketbook was printed in German as part of the ideological campaign aimed at captured German soldiers. It is instructive to reflect on the long-term approach of a Soviet government willing to divert scarce wartime resources for such a project. It suggests that the ten-year captivity of hundreds of thousands of Germans as slave labourers had been foreseen, and that their long-term political indoctrination was considered worthwhile.

These texts, originally for Soviet consumption, also show an interesting development in Stalin's rhetoric. Before the war this had reflected the Party's collectivist dogma, being addressed to 'Comrades, party leaders, soldiers, sailors, commanders, workers, leading workers', and so forth. From his first wartime speech he used an intimate form of address: 'Brothers and sisters' – a familiar phrase to older Russians, since it was employed by Orthodox priests at the beginning of the church liturgy.

(*Opposite, bottom*) Characters from the fonts of a field printing press, and German propaganda leaflets. Printed propaganda, loudspeakers in the front lines, and radio broadcasts were all employed by both sides in the effort to weaken morale and reduce their opponents' will to resist. German field presses used Cyrillic fonts, and their Soviet opposite numbers Latin alphabets, to print this propaganda material and pronouncements to the inhabitants of occupied territories. The examples shown here were found near a Red Army city headquarters next to a German prisoner of war camp; most of the lead slugs had melted, probably after an explosion caused by artillery fire.

The German propaganda leaflets quoted (not always truthfully) German military regulations on how surrendering Russian soldiers were to be welcomed if they chose to join the Wehrmacht. By late 1942 the Nazi regime's racist contempt for Slavic 'sub-humans' was being tempered to some extent by the realistic recognition that they needed every man on their side who would carry a rifle. These leaflets hold out to their readers – for the first time – a vision of a United Europe under a new world order, free of Communists and Jews. They feature General A.A.Vlasov, the commander of the abandoned 2nd Shock Army who had been captured on the Leningrad front in July 1942, and who was sponsored by German Army Intelligence to raise the Russian Liberation Army (ROA) from prisoners and willing ethnic minorities. The leaflets show smiling, well-fed volunteers in brand new uniforms, merrily playing guitars and balalaikas, and recount how 'free' Russian troops are helping with agriculture, industry and construction.

The leaflets claim to serve as safe conduct passes for anyone who approaches German forces in order to change sides. They also appeal to their readers to carry out sabotage against the 'Bolshevik' Red Army.

DOCUMENTS & EPHEMERA

139

DOCUMENTS & EPHEMERA

(**Opposite, top**) *Red Army occupation banknotes for Czechoslovakian and Hungarian territories, 1944. In the absence of functioning civil administrations the advancing Red Army had to provide not only for their own troops and the rising number of prisoners, but to some extent also for the local inhabitants. In Hungary and Czechoslovakia they started to print their own local banknotes without reference to the national banks. The notes, not withdrawn until early 1946, were naturally unbacked by any reserve, but the people had to accept them or face a military court. Consequently, these countries whose infrastructure and economy had been almost totally destroyed suffered from post-war hyper-inflation; by the end of 1946, a* pengo *banknote was in circulation in Hungary with a nominal value of 1 followed by 20 zeros (one hundred quintillion), which purchased a single egg or a box of matches. The cheaply printed banknotes had no consistent typefaces, designs, issuing signature, or sometimes even serial numbers.*

(**Right**) *A high quality hand-painted china plate from a 1930s dinner service marked for the Workers' and Peasants' Red Fleet (Navy), and still in use ten years later.*

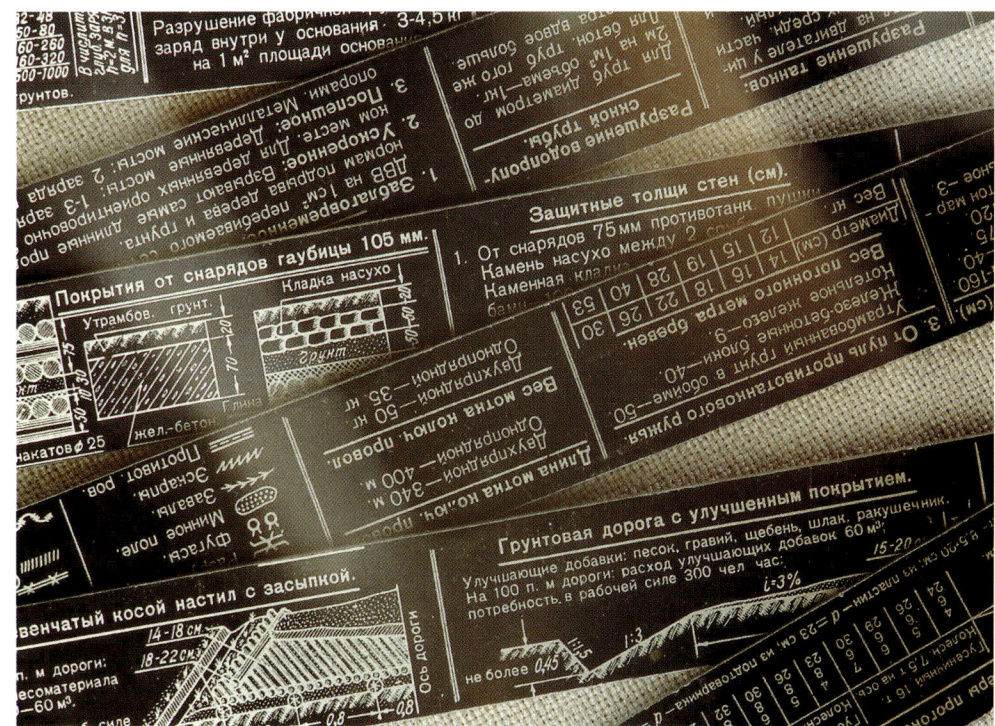

(**Left**) *An engineer officers' metal folding rule made in 1941. Apart from its primary function it is also marked with many kinds of useful information – e.g. tables, angles and standards for both construction and demolition tasks.*

(**Right**) *A medic's Red Cross armband. This has a sewn-on cross; cheaper versions were simply painted. Such brassards were not often used in the front lines; on the Eastern Front neither side tended to respect the Geneva cross, and medical personnel were routinely fired upon.*

(**Opposite, below**) *Typically, items were picked up and personalised by servicemen. The engraving on this German cigarette case records that it was 'collected' in Königsberg, East Prussia, in 1945 by a Soviet pilot.*

DOCUMENTS & EPHEMERA

(Left) Fighters' Calendar *for the year 1944; the December pages give hints on tackling the German Tiger tank (see also page 104). This pocket diary contained propaganda notes as prominently as practical suggestions. Days to remember in December 1944 included the anniversary of the Constitution of Stalin (5 December), with a quotation from the constitution's Paragraph 133: 'It is every Soviet citizens' duty to protect the Motherland.'*

Another important anniversary in December was Stalin's birthday on the 21st (which soldiers would remind one another is the darkest day of the year). The diary also contained inspirational notes on the life of Stalin; extracts from speeches urging the defiance of invaders from such heroes as Alexander Nevski, Suvorov and Kutuzov; and quotations from military regulations.

(Below) This illustration from the Partisan's Companion *handbook reminds readers of perhaps the most basic of all Russian military skills: the proper wrapping of the foot-cloths which were still used instead of socks under the boots. This was a centuries-old Russian folk practice, but the Red Army still insisted on making sure that no recruit had any excuse for not doing it properly. The Soviet soldier was still wearing foot cloths and high boots in 1991.*

(Right) The diary illustrated practical advice on e.g. how to carry and protect weapons, build trenches and apply camouflage; techniques for using compass and map; first aid, water purification, and security regulations to be observed when writing home. This page shows ways of orienting oneself north or south without the benefit of a compass.

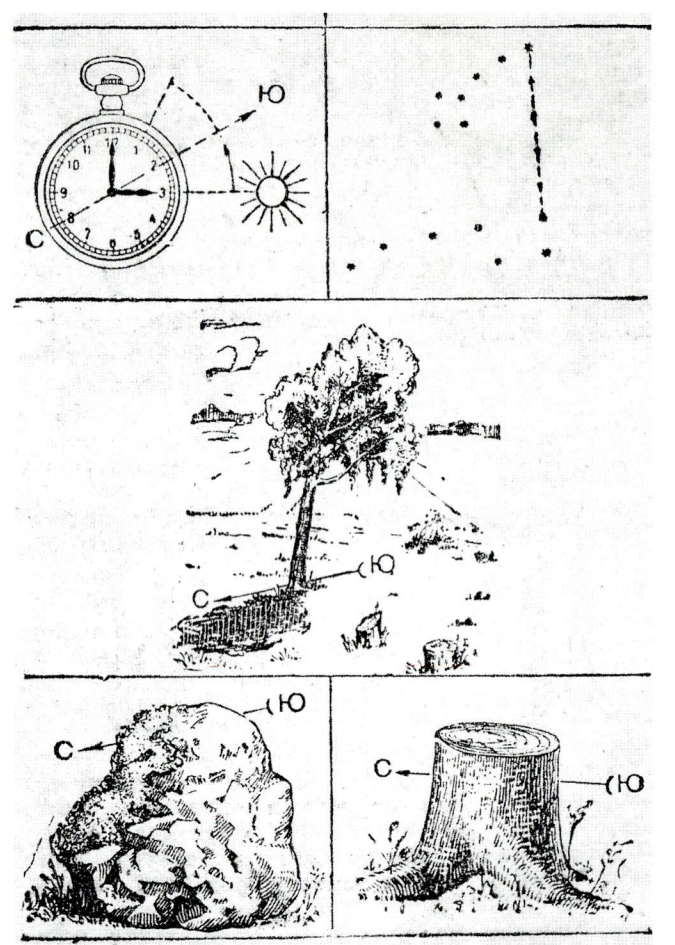

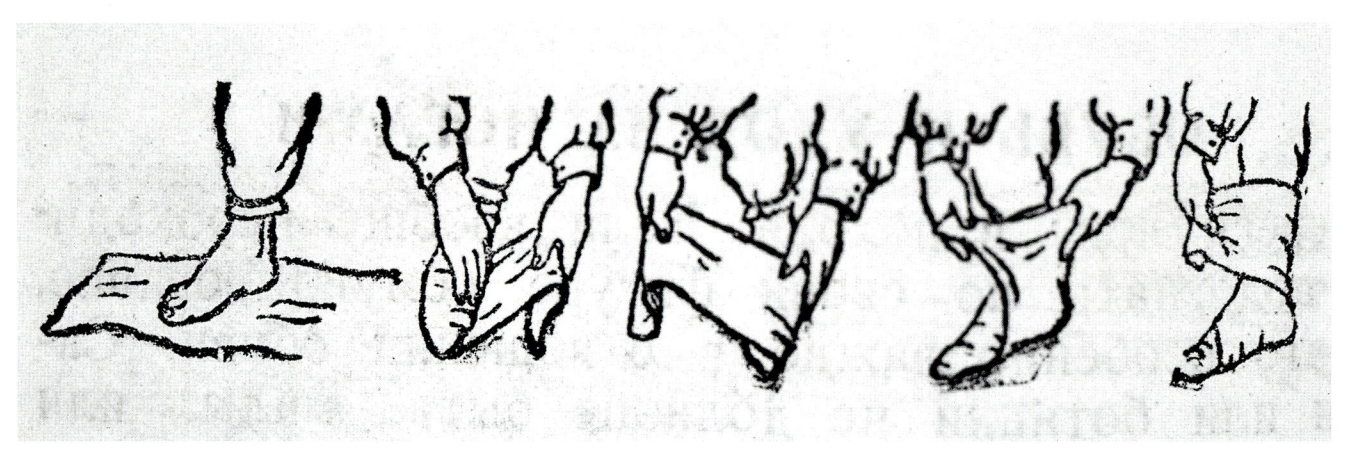

— 142 —

It is often difficult to distinguish wartime from post-war items of Soviet clothing, equipment and small kit. Most World War II designs remained in production until 1955 with only minor changes; cloth items hardly ever had clear date-stamps, and anyway these seldom survived repeated washing.

(Above) Battlefield relics of the Red Army, with some German and Hungarian finds. The siege and battle of Budapest in winter 1944/45 lasted more than two months and left indelible damage on the city; all the great Danube bridges were destroyed, and some buildings still bear bullet holes from World War II (and from the 1956 uprising). In the 1980s it was reported that some buildings still showed on doorways wartime notices chalked by Red Army engineers, for instance MIN NET ('no mines').

(Right) A Red Army button made in Prague, 1945, sewn to a veterinary's tunic. All the resources of liberated or occupied territories were immediately put to the service of the Soviet state.

(Below right) Label from a Red Army officer's cap made in Erfurt, East Germany, in 1952. As war reparations the plant from many German factories was transported to the USSR, and machinery left in place was used to supply the Red Army.

(Below) Red Army and Royal Hungarian Army buttons, found near Budapest after lying a metre apart for 60 years since the battle for the city.

*The grave of an unknown Soviet soldier. Before the defacement
of his stone in 1989, at least his name was recorded.*